THE LAWYER'S GUIDE TO
Increasing Revenue

Unlocking the Profit Potential in Your Firm

Arthur G. Greene

ABA LawPracticeManagementSection

MARKETING • MANAGEMENT • TECHNOLOGY • FINANCE

Commitment to Quality: The Law Practice Management Section is committed to quality in our publications. Our authors are experienced practitioners in their fields. Prior to publication, the contents of all our books are rigorously reviewed by experts to ensure the highest quality product and presentation. Because we are committed to serving our readers' needs, we welcome your feedback on how we can improve future editions of this book.

Cover design by Jim Colao.

Library of Congress Cataloging-in-Publication Data

The Lawyer's Guide to Increasing Revenue: Unlocking the Profit Potential in Your Firm. Arthur G. Greene. Library of Congress Cataloging-in-Publication Data is on file.

ISBN 1-59031-422-0

09 08 07 06 05   5 4 3 2 1

Discounts are available for books ordered in bulk. Special consideration is given to state bars, CLE programs, and other bar-related organizations. Inquire at Book Publishing, American Bar Association, 321 N. Clark Street, Chicago, Illinois 60610.

Contents

Preface

The purpose of this book is to share with lawyers what I consider to be some different and more enduring ideas for improving the bottom line. The recommendations for unlocking a law firm's profit potential are conclusions of mine, based on thirty-seven years of practice, which has included managing a seventy-lawyer firm, establishing and running a two-lawyer firm in which I had the liberty to implement the concepts that I recommend, and advising small and midsized firms on financial issues.

The biggest mistake made by lawyers is to assume that the road to better profits must include reducing costs, increasing hourly rates, and increasing the number of billable hours. These strategies are far too prevalent as our profession faces increased challenges. In most cases, they fail to achieve the desired results, and at the same time they also create additional problems with client satisfaction and lawyer and staff morale.

I have not seen a firm that didn't have untapped potential. The best approach is to recognize and develop that potential for better profits while at the same time benefiting from heightened client satisfaction and improved law firm morale. The goal of the book is to help lawyers achieve that result.

Acknowledgments

I have many friends and colleagues to thank for their help with this book. The active members of the Law Practice Management Section of the ABA have been a source of inspiration and guidance for me in developing the concepts that provide the basis for increasing revenue. Included among those are David Bilinsky, past Chair of the Finance Core Group, along with Steven Campbell and Deborah McMurray, whose participation and advice was essential to crafting the final product. I want to also thank the immediate past and current Publishing Board Chairs, Greg Siskind and Reid Trautz, whose continual support and advice has been invaluable.

I appreciate the efforts of the ABA staff members, who have brought their many talents to developing the project, providing insight on content, editing the words, creating the final product, and promoting the book in the legal marketplace. So to Beverly Loder, Timothy Johnson, and Neal Cox, I say many thanks for all you have done to make this book project successful.

And an important thank you to Kathy Williams-Fortin, a top-notch paralegal who has assisted me for at least two decades. Her careful review and advice on every aspect of this book has made it substantially better than it might have been.

About the Author

Arthur G. Greene was formerly a partner with a large New Hampshire firm, where he practiced law from 1967 until 2000 and served as managing partner for several years during the 1980s. He has now established the firm of Greene Perlow, P.L.L.C., in which he continues his statewide practice in a small-firm setting. He is an adjunct professor at Franklin Pierce Law Center, where he teaches Law Practice Management. Mr. Greene also has a consulting practice that focuses on both practice management and the strategic and financial aspects of maintaining a healthy firm. His consulting involves conducting profitability studies, facilitating retreats, and providing guidance and recommendations on a variety of management topics, including paralegal utilization, attorney/client dynamics, alternative billing methods, and partner compensation.

Think Revenue

"How Can We Do Better Next Year?"

That is the question posed in law firms and neighboring coffee shops each January as lawyers reflect on the financial performance of their firms. Year after year those discussions result in plans for improvement, but as Yogi Berra would say, "It seems like *déjà vu* all over again."

Why do annual plans for improvement, whether formal or informal, miss the mark and not produce significant financial rewards? How can law firms get beyond the superficial efforts that fail to achieve improved results? Why are some firms stuck in a continuing spiral of mediocrity?

A common failing for firms is to devote an inordinate amount of time and energy to expense-reduction efforts to the exclusion of more productive approaches. While extravagant and unnecessary spending should be eliminated from law firm budgets, cost cutting has serious limitations and, if taken to the extreme, can undercut production capacity and law firm morale. In a worst-case scenario, a law firm can exacerbate its problems by relying too heavily on the cost-cutting approach to financial management. No firm has forged its way to long-term success though cost cutting!

On the revenue side, firms that focus their time and energy on adjustments in billable hours and hourly rates also make a mistake. While some firms survived the 1990s by regularly increasing billable-hour requirements and raising their hourly rates, those strategies became self-limiting over time and have resulted in both client unhappiness and a decline in lawyer morale. Cranking up billable hours and hourly rates is not the answer.

Law firms wanting to improve profits need to identify and implement effective revenue approaches and develop a multiyear plan for achieving better financial results. The revenue recommendations presented here are followed by practical step-by-step plans that will result in improved revenue and larger profits with strategies that also focus on maintaining positive attorney-client relationships and healthy law firm environments.

Develop a Revenue Mind-set

1

Lawyers can take satisfaction from the tremendous value they provide to clients through the knowledge, wisdom, and skill they apply to the matter at hand in the form of counseling, negotiating, or litigating. But it is not unusual to hear lawyers lament the fact that while earning a relatively modest hourly rate they have been an important factor in making many of their clients wealthy. Unfortunately for lawyers, profit margins are tightening and the legal marketplace has experienced changes that are making it increasingly difficult to realize fair and adequate financial rewards for the services they render.

This problem is complicated by the fact that most lawyers do not welcome any change in the way they practice law. In response to what is happening around them, lawyers often react by trying to pedal faster and faster to keep up. Blinded by the work at hand, they are not receptive to spending the time necessary to think about what steps to take to improve their profits in the years ahead. To break this pattern and achieve improved profits, the first step is to develop a revenue mind-set.

How to Make a Big Difference

Here is the important concept:

> Increasing revenue, *while maintaining the same expense structure*, is the most powerful approach to improving the firm's bottom line.

Simple math demonstrates that those extra revenue dollars go straight to the bottom line and make a profound impact on partner profits. For example, assume the firm generates $1.5 million annually and that there is a 50-percent profit margin, meaning $750 thousand goes to overhead and the other $750 thousand goes to the partners as compensation or profits.

Annual Revenue	$1,500,000
Expenses	750,000
Partner Profit	750,000

Now, if the firm is able to increase its revenue by 10 percent while maintaining the same cost structure, 100 percent of the additional revenue dollars will go to the partners. Therefore, partner profits would be $900,000.

Annual Revenue	$1,650,000
Expenses	750,000
Partner Profit	900,000

Take a moment to think about what this means. A modest 10-percent increase in revenue produces a 20-percent increase in partner profits. A 15-percent increase in revenue produces a 30-percent increase in partner profits. The payback is good. Those extra dollars can make a big difference to the lifestyle and the satisfaction of the partners.

While there is something to be said for the concept that one has to spend money to make money, caution needs to be exercised before declaring that spending is the solution to a firm's need for increased profits. There are certainly circumstances in which a firm can benefit from spending money on a new initiative; the firm needs to recognize, however, that a plan that increases both revenue and expenses does not necessarily improve profits. In fact, it can have the opposite effect.

Lawyers work long and hard to meet the firm's revenue budget without appreciating how many of those extra dollars slide into their own pockets if there is additional revenue once the overhead has been covered. The lawyers who do appreciate the significance of the extra revenue may be reluctant to push in that direction because they believe that extra revenue requires working longer hours. But nothing is further from the truth. The extra revenue can result from a variety of sources, including better management of the revenue side of the budget, value-based billing methods, improved client satisfaction, and so on. There are almost always significant dollars *that are left on the table* . . . that is, left there for the taking.

Why Cost Approaches Fail

Yes, extravagant and unnecessary spending must be eliminated. However, once those items are removed, the repeated effort to slash costs as a means of meeting financial challenges is an ill-conceived approach to financial management. The vast majority of law firm expenses are either fixed or production-related. The percentage of costs that might be classified as discretionary is low, perhaps in the 20 to 30-percent range. Assuming that some of the discretionary expenses are desirable, the number of dollars available there for savings is small. The available dollars disappear after a year or two of cost cutting, leaving firm management wrestling with the effect of further cuts on the firm's production capability.

Does it make sense to eliminate staff positions if the result is to put more administrative functions on the lawyers and paralegals? Of course not; such an approach would reduce the amount of billable work product. Does it make sense to cut back on the lawyers' continuing legal education? Probably not; improving one's level of expertise is important to increasing revenue production. Does it make sense to cut the marketing budget? Probably not, if there is a revenue problem and the goal is to develop more high-end business. What are the lawyers thinking? It can be so painful to watch a firm struggling with a revenue problem, debating what further costs to cut in order to improve profits!

There are law firms that have actually put themselves out of business by trying to forge their way to success through cost cutting year after year. These firms get to the point where the production capacity provided to the lawyers becomes so low that revenues decrease to the point of no return. It is not a happy sight.

It does not take a rocket scientist or a three-year plan to look at the expense side of a budget and remove unnecessary costs. Once the firm takes a look and makes appropriate adjustments, an attempt to continue to push too hard on the cost side undercuts the possibility of turning the firm around and making it a financially successful organization.

Most firms addressed unnecessary and extravagant costs in the 1990s and have removed them from the firm budget. Lawyers have to move beyond the cost-cutting phase quickly, and recognize the need to focus on revenue in their efforts to create a more successful firm.

Places to Look for Revenue

Now for the good news: there are several places to look for additional revenue potential within an existing law practice.

- ◆ **Increase Billing Realization Rate:** Billing Realization is the percentage of the recorded billable hours that is actually billed to the client. Bills get written down for any number of reasons. Is the firm's billing realization rate 75 percent or 95 percent, or some other number? Whatever the number, there is a good chance it can be improved by 5 percent or more. This can be achieved by determining the causes of the billing write-offs and eliminating them.

◆ **Increase Collection Realization Rate:** Collection write-offs are bills that are submitted to clients and never paid. At some point, when collection seems unlikely, the firm takes a bill out of its receivables column and it becomes a collection write-off. Is the firm's collection realization rate 85 percent or 95 percent, or some other number? This is another area where a reduction in write-offs adds profits to the bottom line.

◆ **Increase Efficiency of Production:** Most lawyers can improve the efficiency of their law practice. The more efficient and productive the lawyer, the more hours during the day are captured as billable hours. One additional hour of productive time a day can make a huge difference in revenue.

> 230 working days @ 5.5 billable hours x $200 = $253,000
> 230 working days @ 6.5 billable hours x $200 = $299,000

The goal is not to have lawyers spend more time in the office, but rather to make better use of the time they are there. Lawyers tend to lose from 20 percent to 40 percent of their potential billable time through poor time-management skills or inadequate support.

◆ **Increase the Profit Margin:** Firms that have clung to hourly billing have seen their profit margins tightened, meaning they have to bill more hours to stay even. Using other value-based billing methods allows a firm to better leverage its expertise and its investment in technology to achieve an improved profit margin on each project.

By improving results in any of these areas, a firm increases revenue production not only in the current year, but also in each succeeding year as long as the improved methods of operation continue. In other words, these are not one-time gains, but continue to provide financial rewards year after year.

But the analysis does not stop there. There are some additional areas for improved revenue that provide one-time gains. For example:

◆ **Billing Turnover Rate:** The billing turnover rate is the average time it takes from the time the work is performed until it is billed. It is usually stated in terms of months, such as 2.1 months. If the firm can improve the time by a half a month, in this case to 1.6 months, then the firm benefits from additional revenue equal to one half of a month's receipts.

◆ **Collection Turnover Rate:** The collection turnover rate is the average time it takes from the time work is billed until it is collected. It is usually stated in terms of months, such as 2.7 months. If the firm can improve the time by a half a month, in this case to 2.2 months, then the firm will benefit from a surge of revenue equal to about one half of a month's revenue.

Unlike the realization rates, the extra revenue flow from an improvement in turnover rates does not continue from year to year. It represents a one-time surge of revenue. On the flip side, it is important to realize that if either of the turnover rates slips in succeeding years, there will be a cash flow shortage. Therefore, it does not make sense to push the turnover rate to a level that cannot be maintained long term.

Other Ways to Improve Revenue

As we continue to move into the twenty-first century, client expectations and client satisfaction loom large as factors in a firm's ability to maximize revenue production. At the same time, experienced lawyers are beginning to better understand the value of the services they provide to clients and are finding better ways to charge clients for that value.

In addition, lawyers are reevaluating the use of leverage in the law firm. Unlike the pyramid concept of the 1970s and 1980s, leverage today does not necessarily involve delegating to large numbers of associates. The new leverage concepts involve improved practice methods and new approaches to billing clients, all of which enable lawyers to treat technology as a profit enhancer, not just an expense.

Increasing hourly rates has been left off the list for now. Too many firms have already pushed their rates to the limit. Further rate increases may adversely affect client relationships and result in problems attracting new business. Similarly, increasing billable hour requirements of hardworking lawyers and paralegals is not a good idea. While capturing more billable hours through better efficiency is important to improved revenue, pushing lawyers by adopting excessively high requirements is not. The goal is to find places to improve revenue within the existing cost structure that do not adversely impact client relationships or lawyer morale.

Revenue, Revenue, Revenue

To summarize, there are three ways to improve law firm profits. They are *revenue, revenue,* and *revenue!* A bad joke, perhaps. Or is it?

Examine the Financial Indicators

2

By examining a series of standard financial indicators, a law firm can track trends and identify the aspects of its operation that may provide a basis for improved revenue.

The process of developing the financial indicators requires data that is normally part of financial, time, and billing software. Most off-the-shelf software programs utilized by smaller firms can produce the same reports that are available to large firms if the programs are configured appropriately. Extra work may be required if the software's capability to produce some reports is not readily apparent. In many situations, law firm administrators need to take advantage of the software company's support line to learn how to configure the software to produce the desired reports. Start by seeing whether the needed information is readily available; if not, determine how to set up the software and input the data required to produce the reports.

Most software programs allow information to be produced on either a firm-wide basis or sorted by practice area or individual. As you work through these financial indicators, give consideration to which reports would be useful if sorted by practice area. In order to achieve that type of analysis, each file must be designated under a particular category. While this may create additional work, it is important to know which practice areas are producing the best results.

The following measures are some of the more common financial indicators that should be tracked.

Profit/Expense Ratio

A primary financial indicator is the ratio of profits to expenses. In that analysis, all dollars going to the partners, including the value of partner fringe benefits, is considered profit and measured against all other expenses. For example:

Revenue	$1,500,000
Expenses	700,000
Partner Profit	800,000
Profit Ratio	53%

There is no magic ratio for firms because there are too many variables. The profit ratios for most firms fall somewhere between 30 percent and 70 percent. Regardless of the percentage, the firm's goal should be to look for ways to improve the profit ratio. Trends are important, so watching how the profit ratio changes over a number of years is also instructive.

All financial software programs provide a profit and loss statement report that shows income, expenses, and net profit or loss for the month, or for any time period. Programs allow income and expenses to be broken down by appropriate categories, which means that meaningful categories need to be created at the outset. These programs also produce reports showing year-to-year comparisons.

For example, the sample below is a simple profit and loss statement showing the results for March and year to date. With most software programs, this report can be run with additional columns showing comparisons to the prior year.

Profit and Loss Statement March 2005		
	March 05	Year to Date
Income		
Legal Fee Income	$98,570	$276,450
Other Income	75	157
Total	$98,645	$276,607
Expenses		
Advertising	1,411	3,500
Bank Service Charges	140	420
Conferences and Seminars	—	—
Contributions	500	500
Credit Card Services	250	750
Dues and Subscriptions	—	200
Professional Liability Insurance	$ 1,250	$ 3,750

Office Expense		
Computers	$ 450	$ 2,345
Postage and Delivery	140	476
Printing and Reproduction	180	375
Supplies	850	2,597
Telephone	479	1,475
Payroll		
Associates	$10,000	$ 30,000
Paralegals	6,750	20,250
Staff	6,200	18,600
Fringe Benefits	3,375	8,850
Payroll Taxes	2,070	6,210
Library	$ 1,238	$ 3,330
Occupancy		
Building Services	$ 625	$ 1,875
Rent	2,575	7,725
Insurance	250	750
Utilities	452	1,450
Professional Services	—	—
Total	$39,185	$115,428
Profit/Loss	$59,460	$161,179

Most U.S. law firms utilize the cash method of accounting, although the accrual system is used in Canada and some other places.

Revenue per Lawyer

Average revenue per lawyer is a number that allows comparisons with industry standards and also helps the firm track changes in its productivity from year to year. Some firms track revenue by lawyer; others track revenue by partner. This report can be run either way, or both ways.

Profit per Partner

Average profit per partner allows for industry comparisons as well as tracking trends in the overall profitability of the firm.

Billing Realization Rate

The billing realization rate is the percentage of recorded billable time that gets billed to clients. The amount that is not billed to clients may have been written off for a variety of reasons. In some cases, it represents time invested that is not well spent; in other situations it is time that cannot be justified based on the intrinsic value of the work or the arrangement with the client. Some lawyers have to write off time due to inefficient work or poor practice methods.

A billing realization rate for one client matter is shown below.

Dollar Value of the Time Invested in the Matter	$1,575
Amount Billed to the Client	1,200
Billing Realization	76%

An average billing realization rate for all of the firm's work can be calculated and tracked year to year. A further level of analysis can be conducted by calculating the billing realization rate for a practice area or for an individual lawyer.

There is no standard rate that all firms should strive to achieve. A billing realization rate of 95 percent is considered good by most standards. A billing realization rate of 85 percent or less is considered problematic. But, regardless of the firm's current rate, the goal should be to improve the rate. Ironically, the lower the realization rate the greater the opportunity for increased revenue. Think about it.

Aged Work-in-Process

The aged work-in-process report shows the value of unbilled work as of the date of the report, broken down into categories of thirty days, sixty days, ninety days, and so on. Some work is billed monthly and other work is billed at conclusion. Obviously the type of work affects the results. If possible, it is helpful to break down the different types of work into separate reports.

This report helps determine whether there is unbilled work that should have been billed. It can also be used to track the investment of time in matters that are not billed monthly such as flat-fee work and contingency work.

Billing Turnover Rate

Billing turnover is the amount of time it takes on average until the work is billed. The information needed to calculate billing turnover is (1) the average billings per month, and (2) the amount of work-in-process on the books at year's end. The billing turnover rate is determined by dividing year-end work-in-process by the average monthly billings.

Example 1

Average Billings per Month	$90,126
Year-end Work-in-Process	251,863
Billing Turnover Rate	
$250,000 divided by $90,000	2.7777 months
Rounded	2.8 months

Example 2

Average Billings per Month	$275,550
Year-end Work-in-Process	425,250
Billing Turnover Rate	
$425,250 divided by $275,550	1.54327 months
Rounded	1.5 months

The turnover rate varies based on the type of work as well as billing practices. Probate work or other areas where it is the practice to collect the fee at the conclusion of the matter causes the average turnover rate to be substantially longer. Similarly, contingency work leads to a much longer time frame. This calculation can be done firm wide, but it is most useful if it is also calculated separately for each practice area.

Collection Realization Rate

The collection realization rate represents the percentage of billed work that is actually collected.

For the purpose of this analysis, it is useful to set an arbitrary time period after which an unpaid bill is considered to be uncollectible. For example, the likelihood of collecting a bill that is over a year old is statistically very low. Carrying uncollectible bills on the accounts-receivable report confuses financial analysis, and thinking that the money may be collected in the days ahead may give the firm a false sense of well-being.

For example, here is the analysis for a firm-wide collection realization rate:

Amount Billed to All Clients	$1,234,000
Amount of Those Bills Collected	1,150,000
Collection Realization Rate	93%

Aged Accounts Receivable

The aged accounts receivable report shows the amount of unpaid client bills, broken down into categories of thirty days, sixty days, ninety days, and so on. The report is used to identify clients with overdue receivables, and to assess the effect of the firm's collection problem on cash flow.

Collection Turnover Rate

Receivables can be considered good news if they are fresh and bad news if they are stale. If the firm has a cash-flow problem, it can be good to know that there are receivables to collect. However, it is important to know whether the aged accounts receivable report paints a healthy picture or a troubled picture of the firm. To make that determination, it is necessary to calculate the collection turnover rate, which is the average time it takes to collect a bill from the day the bill is mailed until the day the cash is received.

    Unfortunately the collection turnover calculation is not intuitive. The information needed for the calculation is (1) the average daily billings, and (2) the year-end amount of the firm's accounts receivable. The collection turnover rate is determined by dividing the year-end accounts receivable by the average daily billings.

    <u>Example 1</u>

Amount of Annual Billings	$825,000
Average Daily Billings $825,000 divided by 365	$2,260
Year End Accounts Receivable	$275,000
Collection Turnover Rate $275,000 divided by $2,260	121.68141 days
Rounded	122 days

    <u>Example 2</u>

Amount of Annual Billings	$825,000
Average Daily Billings $825,000 divided by 365	$2,260
Year End Accounts Receivables	$130,000
Collection Turnover Rate $130,000 divided by $2,260	57.522123 days
Rounded	58 days

Run that calculation for the firm. In the process, take a look at the firm's policy for writing off bad receivables. Some firms are not willing to write off bad debts and the result is that accounts-receivable reports are skewed by either keeping old uncollectible accounts on the report or by writing off accounts receivable too early. Adopt a standard time frame. For example, a reasonable policy might be to write off receivables when they reach an age of twelve months. If there remains a hope of collection, they could be moved to a doubtful-accounts category, thereby keeping them in the system but removing them from active accounts-receivable reports. Whatever you determine for a policy, apply it consistently.

What is an acceptable collection turnover rate? Unfortunately, there is no uniform answer that applies to all firms. In Example 1, the collection turnover rate is 122 days, a dismal performance for almost any firm. However, the collection turnover rate in Example 2 is 58 days, a number more typical of firms that think they are well run.

The collection turnover rate is affected by practice areas, client profiles, geographical location, and the economy. If your firm's results are between 30 days and 60 days it is probably within the range of most firms. However, comparing your firm to those numbers is not the issue. Since there is no uniform standard, the real question is whether your firm's collection turnover rate can be improved. For most firms the answer is yes.

Billable Hours by Timekeeper

A billable hours by timekeeper report permits an evaluation of the number of billable hours for each of the firm's timekeepers. Analyzing where the shortfalls are occurring can help identify workload and practice-area issues that need attention. Also, it can identify lawyers or paralegals whose contribution of billable hours may be deficient due to a lack of work ethic, poor time-recording techniques, or inadequate work load.

Low billable hours on the part of a lawyer or paralegal signals a place where improvement will result in additional revenue. The goal is not to increase billable hour requirements, but rather to identify spots where revenue expectations are falling short through personal timekeeping or practice-management issues.

Billings

The billings report demonstrates the dollar value of billings for the month and the total to date for the year. Most firms report billings by partner or by lawyer. It is also useful to sort and evaluate this billings information on a practice-group basis.

These reports are useful in assessing each lawyer's productivity and delegation skills, as well as the success of each practice group.

Cash

The cash report demonstrates the dollar value of cash collections for the month and the total to date for the year. Cash can be reported for the firm, by partner, by lawyer, and by practice group. These reports are useful in assessing the quality of the clients and the lawyers' success in actually collecting revenue.

Volume or Price

There is one other analysis that can be useful. For a firm that is growing its revenue, it is useful to know whether increased revenue is coming from increased business or increased hourly rates. The idea is that growth is more healthy if the increase is the result of additional business rather than the result of increasing the charge for the same amount of work.

To run that analysis, you need the billable hours, the average hourly rate, and the revenue for the current year and the past year. For the purpose of our analysis, consider the following data:

	2003	2004
Revenue	$790,560	$975,536
Average Rate	$145	$154
Billable Hours	6,202	7,050

To determine the effect of additional business, multiply the increase in billable hours by the prior year's rate, and then get the percentage by dividing that number by the total revenue increase:

$$848 \times \$145 = \$122,960 \text{ divided by } \$184,976 = 66\%$$

To determine the effect of the rate increase, multiply the increase in rate by total hours for the year, and then get the percentage by dividing that number by the total increase in revenue:

$$\$9 \times 7,050 = \$63,450 \text{ divided by } \$184,976 = 34\%$$

In this example, 34 percent of the increased revenue resulted from raising hourly rates and 66 percent of it came from increased business. As you watch trends from year to year, you want to see a healthy portion of the additional revenue coming from increased business.

Establishing the Baseline

The financial indicators provide the data necessary to establish a baseline upon which to track trends in the firm's financial performance. Having the systems in place to develop these reports is essential for properly analyzing the financial health of the firm and for determining the places where improvement can result in enhanced profits. See Appendices A-1 through A-9 for samples of standard reports. The worksheet in Appendix B and on the accompanying CD will assist with calculating the financial indicators for a law firm.

Find Maximum Capacity

3

The revenue capacity of a law firm is deemed to be the amount of money that the firm should be able to generate with its lawyers and paralegals working at their highest and most efficient level given the firm's existing support, present systems, and current technology. It represents the most revenue that the firm might hope for with its present operating structure and practice methods. The firm's capacity should be used as a benchmark to get a sense of how the firm is doing and the extent to which it has unrealized revenue potential.

Revenue capacity has nothing to do with actual revenue or the current performance of the firm. In fact, revenue capacity has subjective elements that are elusive at best. We can, however, get a rough idea of capacity by looking at certain objective information relating to the firm's operation. Once revenue capacity is determined, it can be compared to actual performance for the purpose of finding ways to bring the firm's performance more in line with its capacity.

Lawyers and Paralegals

Lawyers and paralegals are central to a firm's revenue capacity. In the budgeting process, most law firms construct their revenue budget based on standard hourly rates. The same method applies when determining existing revenue capacity.

Start by taking the standard hourly rate of each lawyer and paralegal and multiplying the rate by the anticipated number of billable hours. The hours used in the analysis should be realistic based on the size and location of the firm, the type of work involved, the culture of the firm and, most importantly, historical information about each individual's performance in prior years.

For example:

Lawyer A	1,600 hours x $200 = $320,000
Lawyer B	1,750 hours x $150 = $262,500
Paralegal	1,500 hours x $90 = <u>$135,000</u>
	$717,500 Revenue Capacity

The analysis assumes that the work performed is billed based on hourly rates or, if other billing methods are used, that the hourly rates provide the basis for estimating anticipated revenue. The analysis also assumes that each lawyer and paralegal has an adequate workload, that all billable hours are billed to clients, and that all bills to clients get paid. While these are aggressive assumptions, they do represent a decent goal for the firm, whether or not it is ever achieved.

If the firm's actual revenue exceeds its current revenue capacity based upon this analysis, then the firm is achieving a realization rate in excess of 100 percent. Such a favorable result demonstrates that the firm is operating efficiently and is probably successfully utilizing some value-based billing methods rather than limiting its charges to hourly billing.

To the extent that the firm's actual revenue is lower than its revenue capacity, an analysis can determine whether the shortfall is based on lack of business, a poor work ethic, write-downs of billed time, a collection problem, or some other factor. Identifying the reasons for the shortfall provides the basis for taking corrective action. Think about what each of the following scenarios discloses about the firm's problems:

Scenario 1: Billings are strong. There is plenty of work. People are working hard and there aren't enough hours in the day, but money simply isn't coming in the door.

Scenario 2: Cash flow is a problem. Lawyers and paralegals are busy, but find that it is impossible to bill clients for all of the time invested in the projects. At billing time, there are write-downs to bring the amount of the bill into line with the value of the service or the expectation of the client.

Scenario 3: The firm cannot meet its financial obligations as they come due. Lawyers and paralegals are failing to meet their billable hour expectations. Work tends to expand to fill available time and people seem to be busy with the work they have.

Each scenario points to a different cause for the shortfall in revenue. The brief descriptions above may suggest the answer to the problem, but an analysis of the financial indicators is necessary to verify with clarity the nature of the problem and the needed corrective action.

The worksheet in Appendix C guides the process of determining a firm's revenue capacity. The following chapters provide the tools for determining the reason for any revenue shortfall, and a process for identifying how to prioritize plans for improvement.

For additional information on paralegals and law firm profitability, see *Paralegals, Profitability, and the Future of Your Law Practice*, by Arthur G. Greene and Therese A. Cannon, published by the American Bar Association Law Practice Management Section.

Create a Scorecard

4

Before starting an effort to improve revenue, you need to create a scorecard to help with the analysis.

To demonstrate the scorecard approach, assume a typical small firm of seven partners, three associates, and five paralegals. The hourly rates for partners is $200, for associates $150, and for paralegals $90. The firm expects 1,600 billable hours from its partners, 1,700 billable from its associates, and 1,500 billable hours from its paralegals.

The firm's revenue capacity as described in Chapter 3 is set out below:

Financial Indicator	Firm Capacity	This Year's Results	Next Year's Goal	Next Year's Results	Following Year's Goals
Revenue	3,680,000				
Expenses	****				
Partner Profit	****				
Profit Ratio	****				
Revenue per Lawyer	368,000				
Revenue per Partner	525,000				
Profit per Partner					
Hours	23,800				
Hours per Partner	1,600				
Hours per Associate	1,700				
Hours per Paralegal	1,500				
Billing Realization	100%				
Billing Turnover	****				
Collection Realization	100%				
Collection Turnover	****				

The first column on the scorecard represents the revenue capacity based on the firm's billable hour goals, standard hourly rates, and 100-percent realization. It is the starting point.

Then enter the most recent full year's results in the next column for comparison.

Financial Indicator	Firm Capacity	This Year's Results	Next Year's Goal	Next Year's Results	Following Year's Goals
Revenue	3,680,000	2,375,758			
Expenses	****	1,350,000			
Partner Profit	****	1,025,750			
Profit Ratio	****	43%			
Revenue per Lawyer	368,000	237,575			
Revenue per Partner	525,000	339,394			
Profit per Partner		146,535			
Hours	23,800	22,670			
Hours per Partner	1,600	1,475			
Hours per Associate	1,700	1,625			
Hours per Paralegal	1,500	1,550			
Billing Realization	100%	80%			
Billing Turnover	****	2.3 mo			
Collection Realization	100%	85%			
Collection Turnover	****	3.2 mo			

The scorecard reflects a revenue shortfall of $1,304,242, or about 35 percent of the firm revenue capacity. We can also tell that the portion of the shortfall related to low billable hours is $186,250 of that amount. Although these are real dollars, it is a fairly modest amount compared to other factors. The analysis shows that the real action is in the realization categories. The 80-percent billing realization accounts for $698,750 of the shortfall—and that is big money. And the 85-percent collection realization accounts for an additional $419,242 of the shortfall.

While the results look bleak, there is good news. This firm can do much better. The scorecard identifies where the opportunities exist. Start by looking for places to increase revenue without increasing costs.

Billing Realization

The sample firm has a shortfall of $698,750 due to its 80-percent billing realization. Looking at individual bills may show that small amounts of time have been written off, but those small amounts have added up to a large amount. The goal should be to recoup a portion of that shortfall. For every 1-percent improvement in the billing realization rate, the firm will receive an additional $34,937 in revenue. A 5-percent improvement will result in additional revenue of $174,687.

Collection Realization

The sample firm has a shortfall of $419,242 due to its 85% collection realization. For every 1-percent improvement, there will be additional revenue of $27,949. A 5-percent improvement will result in additional revenue of $139,747.

Hours

The low billable hours has created a shortfall of $186,250. Add 50 hours (about an hour a week) to the partners requirements and revenue will increase by $70,000, assuming it is billed and collected. Add 50 hours to the associates requirements, and revenue will increase by $22,500.

Billing and Collection Turnover Rates

Billing and collection turnover rates are a little different. Improvement in those rates results in one-time rewards and is not something that keeps paying year after year. There is a surge of additional revenue during the year in which the improvement takes place. Once a better turnover rate is established, the revenue levels off to a more normal flow. For example, the firm bills approximately $200,000 a month and collects about $168,000 a month. By improving either turnover rate by half a month, there will be a surge of additional revenue of about $84,000. It can make an important difference for a firm that has cash flow problems. Keep in mind, however, that should the turnover rate slip back in the future, there will be a cash flow loss during any given time period of that same amount.

Setting the Goals

The sample firm should set the following goals for next year:

- ◆ Improve the collection turnover rate from 3.2 months to 2.7 months.
- ◆ Improve the billing realization by 3 percent, moving it from 80 percent to 83 percent.

- ◆ Improve the collection realization by 2 percent, from 85 percent to 87 percent.
- ◆ Get closer to the hours goal by achieving an additional 50 billable hours for each associate.
- ◆ Get closer to the hours goal by achieving an additional 50 billable hours for each partner.

Now, assume the goals for next year are achieved and fill in the goals column on the scorecard.

Financial Indicator	Firm Capacity	This Year	Next Year's Goal	2nd Year Out	3rd Year Out
Revenue	3,680,000	2,375,758	2,972,750		
Expenses	****	1,350,000	1,350,000		
Partner Profit	****	1,025,750	1,622,750		
Profit Ratio	****	43%	54%		
Revenue per Lawyer	368,000	237,575	297,275		
Revenue per Partner	525,000	339,394	424,678		
Profit per Partner		146,535	231,821		
Hours	23,800	22,670	23,450		
Hours per Partner	1,600	1,475	1,525		
Hours per Associate	1,700	1,625	1,675		
Hours per Paralegal	1,500	1,550	1,550		
Billing Realization	100%	80%	83%		
Billing Turnover	****	2.3 mo	2.3 mo		
Collection Realization	100%	85%	87%		
Collection Turnover	****	3.2 mo	2.7 mo		

The goals are intentionally modest. Yet the profits per partner increased from $146,535 to $231,821. That is an average increase in compensation per partner of over $70,000. This analysis demonstrates the power of focusing on the revenue side of the law firm budget.

It would be realistic to plan for similar improvement during the following year, with the exception of the additional $84,000 due to the half-month improvement in collection turnover, which is a one-time event.

This looks pretty hopeful on paper. And the goals in the example for improving the financial indicators are set realistically low, at a level that is likely to be achieved by any firm. A blank scorecard is in Appendix D and is on the accompanying CD.

Learn the Secrets of Achieving Better Revenue

A revenue mindset equips the lawyer to take an enlightened look at management concepts and plan for changes that improve both revenue and profits. The goal in all of this must be to use that revenue focus to employ strategies that improve the lawyer-client relationship and have a positive effect on lawyer morale. Improving lawyer revenue is not inconsistent with improving client satisfaction. In fact, they go hand in hand.

While not obvious on the surface, client expectations represent a significant factor in many revenue-related issues. Although collection problems and billing write-offs may not emerge until the end of the engagement, underlying problems can usually be traced back to the client intake process and the expectations created at that time.

The best way to assure good revenue flow is to create realistic expectations during client intake, and then satisfy those expectations by performing the services in an effective and efficient manner. The expectations set in the initial conference include (1) the legal process involved, (2) the range of likely outcomes, (3) the length of the proceeding, and (4) the amount and timing of the legal fees to be incurred. While a written fee agreement is important, standard agreements are not intended to provide the detail necessary to effectively manage the client expectations.

Then, looking internally, the law firm needs to understand that times have changed, and there is a difference between leverage employed in the 1980s and leverage that works in today's environment. Leveraging through a pyramid structure of high partner-associate ratios has faded into the history books as a legend from the past. The new leverage for small and mid-sized firms focuses on the lawyers' expertise and wisdom in specialized practice areas, supported by the use of value-based billing methods, the application of state-of-the-art technology as a profit factor, and the expanded use of paralegals.

It is this combination of client satisfaction through properly managed expectations, and the law firm's effective internal management of the work through the use of modern leverage techniques that leads to maximizing revenue and profits.

It All Starts at the Beginning

5

Question: What is the best starting point for improving revenue in a law firm?

Answer: Client expectations.

How many lawyers would have answered "client expectations"? Not many. Yet, as underrated as this concept has been with lawyers, it represents a critical factor in improving revenue production.

Think about it. When the client leaves the lawyer's office after the first visit, there are expectations that guide the client's thinking in the days that follow. Hopefully, those expectations are based on what the lawyer has said during that first meeting. However, in some cases, the expectations may be based on what the client *thought* he or she heard. And, for any matters not discussed, the client's expectations are based on preconceived impressions. Any attempt to add to or adjust those expectations later will be difficult, or perhaps impossible.

The expectations set at that initial client meeting include

- ◆ How the legal process works
- ◆ How long the legal process takes
- ◆ What the plan is for addressing the legal issue at hand
- ◆ How the matter is staffed
- ◆ What the range of likely results will be
- ◆ What the overall cost of the legal services will be

- How the services are billed
- When payment of the legal fees is expected
- What happens if fees are not paid when they are due

No other factor is more important to revenue flow than satisfied clients whose expectations are met in all regards. Any failure to establish appropriate expectations at the beginning results in client dissatisfaction, and ultimately in a disruption or delay in payment of legal fees. On the other hand, satisfied clients whose expectations are met are more likely to recognize the value of the services and feel the need to pay their legal fees promptly.

Client Intake

A client who is well informed, engaged in the process, and who sees the matter proceeding in accord with expectations is more inclined to make timely payment for those services. Clients who receive bills for legal fees that are in amounts that they anticipate are prepared to pay for those services. It is a client who is surprised by the amount of a bill or confused by the process who is more apt to leave the legal bill in the pile on the desk.

Think about client intake in your firm. The answer to the questions listed below will help assess where improvement is necessary.

Are all of the firm's current clients appropriate for the firm? Every firm needs to understand what types of clients and cases should be accepted by the firm. Get beyond thinking that more business is always better. The idea that no client should be turned away is problematic. Working for a nonpaying client may make a lawyer feel busy and productive, but may prevent the lawyer from landing a lucrative case because of lack of time for marketing activities.

Make an evaluation of the client, not just the client's case. Does the client have the resources and willingness to support the cost of the legal matter going forward? Never be reluctant to turn the client away if there is a significant reason for concern. Do not overlook the typical warning signs.

Do the firm's clients have reasonable expectations? The client with unrealistic expectations or a lack of understanding of the risks involved and the range of likely outcomes is more likely to become an unhappy client. How well are the firm's lawyers doing in setting reasonable expectations at the initial client meeting, and actively managing those expectations throughout the representation?

Do the lawyers understand the client's objectives and are they able to create and communicate a plan designed to achieve those objectives? At times, the client's true objective is not as it may seem. The lawyer needs to develop a plan for sharing with the client that explains how the objective will be achieved. Making up the plan along the way is not a good alternative.

Does the value of the services delivered to clients seem reasonably consistent with the amount of the legal fees charged? Do the clients start out with realistic understandings of the cost of the services to be performed? Do the clients at the outset have the information necessary to make decisions based on a risk-benefit analysis? If the lawyers provide services of limited value for hourly fees to be determined later, there is a possibility that on receiving bills for the legal fees, clients may regret having decided to go forward.

Clients focus on the most favorable interpretation of any legal fee estimate they hear. Give a range of possible fees and the client is going to remember the lower number. Many collection problems are the result of billings where the amounts ended up exceeding the expectations of the clients.

Do all clients sign fee agreements that adequately describe the financial relationship? Every fee arrangement should be in writing. The fee agreement should specifically state that failure to pay in a timely manner is unacceptable. Unless the payment requirements are spelled out, it is relatively easy for clients to come up with plausible explanations for delayed payment.

Do all clients receive confirmation in writing of the plan for going forward, the range of possible results, and a clear understanding of the costs? Go beyond the executed fee agreement. Put the expectations discussed in the initial consultation in writing. Take every opportunity to reinforce those expectations.

Realistic answers to these questions are important to understanding how client expectations may be affecting the flow of revenue into your firm. A comprehensive plan to improve client intake and better manage client expectations is the starting point for improving a firm's revenue production.

Find the Magic: Payments by Return Mail

6

$\mathbf{A}$ good start with a client is just that—a good *start*. Nothing more. The next goal is to make certain that the client continues to be satisfied with the service. Surveys suggest that the expression of concern by a lawyer is more important to most clients than the results achieved or the amount of the fee. There is a real message here. Lawyers need to care and to show concern on a regular basis.

Magic? It may seem a bit supernatural, but it is not all that hard to get return mail payments from most clients. All it takes are clients with realistic expectations and lawyers who meet those expectations while regularly showing concern for the clients.

> Think back to some of your best client relationships. What do you remember about them? It may be that you remember that payments of your legal fees came back by return mail. The bill was hardly out the door, and there was the check! It was probably so unusual that the immediate payment continues to stand out in your mind. It is also likely that the prompt payment of your fee didn't go unnoticed. You began to treat that client a little better than the slow-pay clients. You probably returned that client's telephone calls more promptly than the others. And you may have tended to lowball the time when filling out your timesheets. The client frequently expressed appreciation for

the services you rendered and you probably expressed thanks for the prompt payment. It was a good situation all around.

What was it that caused the client to pay so promptly? Most likely, the client understood the process and had realistic expectations as to outcome and cost. You had done a good job at the initial client meeting and the case had progressed as expected. To the extent there were any changes from what was discussed, you kept the client involved and gave advance warning of those changes. The client was satisfied and appreciated your services.

Hopefully, the client leaves the initial client conference with a complete and realistic set of expectations, as well confidence with the lawyer and with the plan for going forward. The relationship is off to a good start. Unfortunately, however, after that good start it is all too easy for the lawyer to lose the confidence of the client. Let's count some of the ways this can happen. The lawyer can

- ◆ Fail to return a telephone call promptly
- ◆ Be late with a promised document
- ◆ Overlook a promise to do something
- ◆ Delay giving the client bad news
- ◆ Forget to tell the client about something
- ◆ Send a bill that surprises the client

These events may seem minor to the lawyer who is simply trying to balance the demands of a busy practice. To the client, the failure is considered to be a defining event.

The Consumer Client

Consumer clients are usually unfamiliar with the legal process and the work of lawyers. They may not have needed to seek legal services in the past, but they have undoubtedly heard horror stories from friends and relatives who have had bad experiences with lawyers. This client has tried to avoid lawyers, and may land at the lawyer's door with reluctance and as a last resort.

The first challenge is to overcome the client's concerns and build the client's confidence that the lawyer will take care of the matter appropriately and for a predictable and fair fee. The first meeting is so critical to the client's comfort level. Of course the client needs to understand what will happen and how much it will cost, but the client also needs to feel that the lawyer will be giving special attention to the problem. The client needs to feel treated as a person, not a file. Regardless of the discussion at that first meeting, the client will be watching for evidence that their confidence is well placed.

The Business Client

Many of these same concerns apply to the sophisticated business client, although there may be additional factors involved. The business client may or may not understand the legal process. Assuming some level of understanding, the business client is looking to delegate the problem to the lawyer and get the problem solved. The goal for the business client is to move the worry to someone else's desk.

For the contact person from a large organization, an additional role for the outside lawyer is to make the contact look good in the process, if possible.

With the business client, guard against

- Failing to alert the company contact to downside risk
- Making the company contact look bad by failing to keep that person up to date
- Changing course without a prior discussion
- Submitting a bill that is unexpected in amount
- Delaying the delivery of bad news

Remember, the lawyer has a double agenda—solve the problem and make the contact person look good in the process.

Client Communications as a Tool

As the matter proceeds, client communication becomes critical. There are several key ingredients:

- Keep the client informed of what you are doing.
- Contact the client periodically, regardless of what is happening.
- Alert the client to any changes in the plan or the risks.
- Alert the client ASAP to anything that might affect the amount of the fee.
- Deliver bad news immediately.
- Return phone calls within two hours or have your assistant return the call and tell the client when you will be available.
- Set aside time in the evening or on weekends to return pending phone calls.

◆ Make certain the work descriptions in your bill properly reflect the value of the services rendered.

It is incredibly easy to do something that disappoints a client and cause them to lose confidence in the lawyer or the process. That loss of confidence is to be avoided at all costs.

Certainly, clients need to be informed of all significant events or anything that requires a change of course. If something comes up that disrupts the expectations set at the beginning of the case, the lawyer needs to address the change with the client immediately. The client should be involved in any decision-making that is required, particularly if the change results in additional costs.

For those matters billed each month, the lawyer can use the billing process to communicate with the client. An itemized bill is an excellent place to demonstrate to the client the value being delivered. To use the bill for that purpose, the lawyer has to guard against time entries describing mechanical processes rather than bills demonstrating the value delivered. A well-crafted bill can go a long way in assuring that the client appreciates the value of the services received.

An Art, Not a Science

Yes, perhaps magic *is* the right word. But it doesn't take a magician. All it takes is a lawyer who knows how to take care of clients. Keeping clients content is an art, not a science. It is not the lawyer with the highest grades, nor is it the lawyer who performs the best legal work who keeps clients happy. It is the lawyer who cares. Or more to the point, it is the lawyer whose clients perceive a caring attitude.

Achieving payment of legal fees by return mail is within reach for all lawyers. It may seem like magic, but what it takes is outstanding service and a concern for the clients.

Understanding Twenty-First Century Leverage

7

Remember the pyramid concept? The law firm pyramid was synonymous with leverage in the 1960s and 1970s. Some of the largest firms were boasting huge profits based on high partner-associate ratios. Hourly billing was surging into the forefront as the predominant billing method, and firms that could generate the necessary business were hiring associates and setting them to work cranking out those hours.

The Collapse of the Pyramid

What happened to the pyramid? Well, as with most things, time has brought change. The foundation of the pyramid was eroded in the 1990s by large increases in starting salaries for the top law school graduates. While it was the megafirms in the largest cities that first made those upward adjustments, a ripple effect throughout the profession caused a significant increase in starting salaries in all but the smallest firms in the most remote communities. With those larger salaries came higher hourly rates for new lawyers.

Sophisticated clients were facing financial pressures of their own and began scrutinizing their bills with more care than in the past. They engaged audit companies to review the bills. They established guidelines setting out what they would pay for and what they would not pay for. These same clients became increasingly unwilling to pay high hourly rates for the work of relatively inexperienced associates. They perceived that they were paying for training, which in many cases was an accurate assessment. In a strange twist, they were much more willing to pay the high hourly rates for partner work and looked with favor on the partners being supported by well-qualified paralegals.

As this was happening, law firms were needing to increase hourly rates and billable hour goals to keep up with increasing expenses. While this simple mathematical approach to law firm management may have helped some firms stay profitable through the changing times of the 1980s and 1990s, it was not to succeed in the long run.

While some large firms continue to leverage associates, the trend for most lawyers is to rethink leverage in order to identify new ways to create improved revenue that are more in line with the business practices of this new world.

Leveraging Expertise

Ironically, as clients have become less willing to pay to have a matter handled by inexperienced associates, they are more willing to pay high fees for the experienced go-to lawyers in any particular field. By being able to charge a premium for their expertise, the best lawyers are able to leverage their own experience and wisdom.

While commodity legal work will always be price-sensitive, the work of lawyers with high levels of expertise will not be price-sensitive. In the present marketplace, the goal for most lawyers should be to develop a reputation in their community for being an expert, or better yet to be the go-to person for a particular type of matter. Once that status is achieved, lawyers can leverage their own knowledge to achieve greater profits.

However, it is difficult to leverage a lawyer's expertise to best advantage in matters that are billed by the hour. Higher rates can make a difference, but they do not capture the true value of a lawyer's expertise. As a result, lawyers are exploring and adopting alternative, value-based fee methods.

Value-Based Fee Methods

Every service has an intrinsic value to the client. If there is much to be gained, the value of the service to the client tends to be large. If the anticipated gain is small, then value of the service to the client is limited.

Hourly billing is not intuitive to most clients, particularly those accustomed to budgeting and making decisions based on cost-benefit analyses. This hourly billing problem is compounded by the fact that most clients do not understand the legal process and therefore cannot easily relate hours to the cost of the services.

Client dissatisfaction is usually found in matters involving significant hourly charges that exceed the intrinsic value of the client services provided. Unfortunately, most firms base their revenue budgets on expected billable hours (which are cranked pretty tight), allowing the lawyers little or no flexibility to adjust their charges to take into account the value of the services to clients.

Lawyers need to take the time to understand the value of the services to the clients and to reevaluate their billing methods in order to find ways for their billing to better reflect the intrinsic value of the services they provide. In that analysis, lawyers need to recognize the factors that need to be considered. For example, a fair fee will normally

- ◆ reflect the client's perception of the value of the services performed
- ◆ offer the client predictability of the fee
- ◆ reward the lawyer for efficiency and productivity
- ◆ provide the lawyer with a return on the investment in technology
- ◆ where appropriate, include a sharing of risk

The hourly fee method is often not the best approach. Lawyers need to understand the broad range of possible fee arrangements in order to effectively explore the options and select the one that best fits a particular situation. There is no one fee method that fits all circumstances.

Technology

Each technological advance has the potential to make lawyers more efficient and more cost effective. With increased competition, law firms that do not take advantage of technological advances are at a distinct disadvantage.

For law firms, however, technology is a mixed bag. Law firms struggle to live with it while at the same time they can't live without it. Technology managers are forever working with issues of cost justification, implementation, lawyer buy-in, training, and computer crashes. For all the problems, technology has improved many aspects of client service and law firm operations.

But wait a minute! Where are the rewards for the lawyer? Lawyers are making huge initial investments of money and are also reinvesting to upgrade on a regular basis. How do lawyers recover the costs of that investment?

Technology has to be something more than an expense item. How do the lawyers benefit from improved efficiencies? Shouldn't the lawyers who take the time and effort to become more efficient and effective receive some reward for the effort?

So, who is benefiting from the technology? The answer is simple. If the law firm is billing by the hour, the clients benefit. The lawyers receive no direct benefit. But for work that is billed on flat fees, it is the lawyers who benefit from the improved use of technology. Similarly, lawyers who handle contingency cases benefit from technology. The problem in most firms is that the vast majority of legal work is still billed by the hour.

Theoretically, additions in overhead should be covered by increased hourly rates. However, in most legal markets competition has not allowed hourly rate adjustments that reflect the additional cost of technology. Many firms have given up and are simply accepting technology as a cost of doing business.

The real solution is for firms to move away from hourly rate billing and employ alternative billing methods. If the fees are set on other grounds, lawyers have the potential to share in the benefits realized from the improved use of technology.

Leveraging with Paralegals

Clients have enthusiastically embraced the role of paralegals in the delivery of legal services. As career employees who are narrowly focused, paralegals are well qualified to perform a wide range of services under the supervision of lawyers. Unlike associates who are working their way through the learning curve while waiting to be partners, properly managed and qualified paralegals are able to help lawyers provide better client service at a lower cost while providing improved profits for the law firm.

Over the past thirty years, the practice of law has become more difficult and complex. Lawyers have found it necessary to handle a larger volume of work, which produces greater pressures and a higher level of intensity. There seems to be less time for detail and less time to attend to issues of client comfort. As a result, both the quality of legal work and client satisfaction have been at risk. Enter stage left—paralegals, who are trained to be thorough and good at detail, and tend to be both available to clients and good at attending to client comfort.

The revenues produced and the costs associated with maintaining a paralegal varies depending upon the location and the type of practice. However, the following tabulation reflects a breakdown of paralegal costs in typical communities:

Salary	$45,000
Fringe Benefits	10,000
One-third Secretarial Position	15,000
Share of Other Overhead	<u>10,000</u>
Total Cost of Maintaining Paralegal	$80,000

For the purpose of this analysis, revenue potential is determined by multiplying the paralegal's hourly rate times the billable hours anticipated. A rate of $85 an hour times 1,500 hours equals a revenue potential of $127,500. To shift from potential revenue to actual revenue, a factor representing write-offs and uncollectible fees must be applied. Assuming a factor of 10 percent, we compare revenues of $114,850 with costs of $80,000, leaving anticipated profits in the vicinity of $34,750. In actual practice, the amount of profit varies widely and depends upon the qualifications of the paralegal, the experience of the paralegal, the billing rate, and the firm's cost structure.

Move into the Twenty-First Century

Lawyers need to move beyond the pyramid structure of the 1980s and begin to look at some leverage concepts that are more attuned to the present legal environment. Begin by developing and promoting what the market is looking for—high levels of expertise. Then take a look at how that expertise can be supported and leveraged by the expanded use of paralegals, a shift to value-based billing methods, and the transformation of a firm's technology into a profit center.

Let Your Clients Do the Marketing

8

The preceding chapters focus on how to improve revenue with an existing client base, and the information there applies to the many firms with sufficient client work. In this chapter, think about how the previous discussions can result in a client-based marketing strategy.

It is common for law firms with reasonably satisfied clients to get at least 50 percent of their new work from returning clients or referrals from existing or former clients. Satisfied clients tell their friends and business acquaintances about their lawyers. Perhaps they are motivated by the all too many complaints heard on the street about lawyers. Regardless of the reason, satisfied clients do like to "brag" about their lawyers and refer others to them.

There is a huge marketing potential within a law firm's existing client base. If a firm properly manages expectations, communicates well, and charges fair value-based fees, its clients can become a significant factor in generating new work for the firm. Simply put, satisfied clients are the most effective form of advertising.

Time, Money, and Energy

Think about it. How many advertising dollars does it take to land a new client? What kind of personal energy and effort is involved in attracting a new client? How long does it take? These are all good questions. The answers, of course, are that it takes a fair amount of money, and a lot of energy and time.

All of this leads to the conclusion that there is much to be gained by taking good care of existing clients and priming them to do the marketing for the firm. Perhaps it is not unrealistic to set a goal that all new work comes from existing clients and referrals from them. To accomplish this consider adopting the following rules.

Rule 1: Protect Existing Client Relationships

- ◆ Always appear pleased to hear from clients. If they apologize for "bothering you," set them straight by letting them know it is never a bother.
- ◆ Respond as quickly as possible to any message or request. Apologize profusely for the delay in getting back to them, if it takes more than an hour or two.
- ◆ Respond to concerns and complaints by making things right as soon as humanly possible. Never let issues fester with clients. Always work to turn a negative situation into a positive event.
- ◆ Consider giving clients a cell-phone number and e-mail address. Most clients respect private time and in fact are reluctant to contact you after hours. You will be scoring big points for having provided them with 24-7 access, and most clients never use it.

Rule 2: Make It Easy for Existing Clients to Deliver More of Their Business

- ◆ Show an interest in the clients' families and businesses. Take some time, clearly off the clock, to nurture the relationship. Take clients to lunch. Ride together on out-of-town trips. Seek them out at social events or community activities. Make clients feel important.
- ◆ Make house calls. Agree to meet clients at home or at work from time to time. Lawyers underutilize this approach, but a lot can be learned by meeting on the clients' home turf.
- ◆ Encourage clients to talk about any potential issues they expect to face and don't charge them for the discussion. This often results from the lawyer making inquiries as simple as "How is it going?"

Rule 3: Distinguish Your Firm from the Others

- ◆ Show genuine concern for clients. Most lawyers do not appreciate how little effort it takes to distinguish themselves from other lawyers. Your competition probably gets pretty low grades in this category.
- ◆ Communicate with clients often. A regular flow of communication creates a bond between lawyer and client that is missing with lawyers who only communicate when they decide it is necessary.
- ◆ Provide value-based billing. Talk openly with clients about the legal fees. Offer alternatives and describe the reason for the various choices. Let clients have a say in how the fees are billed.
- ◆ Look for ways to be different from other lawyers. Find ways to change your methods of practice that set you apart in the eyes of potential clients. You are only limited by your imagination.

Rule 4: Make Existing Clients Proud to Refer Clients to You

- ◆ Do a good job for the new clients so the clients who made the referral look good.
- ◆ Always go out of your way to thank clients for any referral or for any kind words.

There are plenty of marketing books available that identify and evaluate a variety of approaches to attaining new business. Few of them give more than lip service to the importance of existing client relationships. While it may be useful to create some target markets and conduct traditional marketing and advertising, don't forget to solidify the foundation—the existing client base.

Realize that by focusing on the revenue-enhancing measures recommended in this book, an unintended benefit is that existing clients may play a larger role in producing new clients for the firm. The price is right. Let your clients do the marketing!

A Step-by-Step Guide for Improving Revenue

Why is it that lawyers spend so little time working on the management of their practices? Most lawyers invest substantial amounts of time and energy on their clients' pursuits, often allowing the clients to achieve new levels of financial success. Yet, lawyers may feel unrewarded for their contributions, based on the profits reflected by their law firm's bottom line.

Yes, most lawyers have an aversion to business aspects of their profession. Those same lawyers would have been more comfortable practicing in the 1870s. Change comes hard for lawyers. And, getting lawyers to dedicate time to their own business methods in order to achieve a better level of financial success is a hard sell.

For those lawyers who do recognize the need to manage their own practice methods, their approach is often superficial, scattered, and lacking in the necessary follow-through. Too often, the plan for financial improvement is limited to cutting costs, raising hourly rates, or pushing for an increase in billable hours. There is no other profession, or business, that pays so little attention to the underlying issues of revenue production methods.

Part III will provide a step-by-step guide to an integrated plan for improving revenue. Avoid the temptation to try for a quick fix. Don't adopt a "Band-Aid® approach" to underlying problems. A collections problem is not for lack of a collection policy. Rather, it reflects on the total operation of the firm and requires the adoption of an integrated approach to fixing each component that is adversely affecting revenue. To use a construction analogy, repair the sagging structural roof timbers before applying new roof shingles.

Look at client intake, fee agreements, client service, and practice methods before deciding how to proceed. The chapters that follow provide an orderly process to follow with regard to each area of concern.

Set in Place the Key Ingredients to Improved Revenue Flow: The Client Intake Process

9

Let's start at the beginning. There is a direct correlation between that initial client meeting and the success of the relationship that follows. The lawyer needs to make a good decision about whether to represent the client. In the process of accepting the client, the lawyer needs to be sure the client has realistic expectations as to the process, the likely outcome, and the cost.

Accepting a client should not be based on an *ad hoc* decision made impulsively at the time of the initial conference. The firm should have a good set of client intake policies and procedures to guide the process. Consider the following steps in developing such policies and procedures.

Step 1: Know Which Clients the Firm Wants

This takes some forethought. Decide on the clients and the cases that the firm wants and then develop policies that help the lawyers make good intake decisions. Always remember that problem clients who fail to pay for their legal services are client intake mistakes.

◆ First, learn from past mistakes. Evaluate the firm's current roster of problem clients and assimilate the information in order to develop an understanding of the types of cases and clients to avoid in the future. Regardless of the firm's need to generate more business, it is rarely worthwhile to fill up one's day by taking on clients who later do not pay for their services.

◆ In developing the policies, decide on the practice areas the firm will serve and require that the lawyers limit their practices to those areas. The most profitable work always comes from the practice areas in which the lawyers have developed a level of expertise. Dabbling in unfamiliar areas of the law is usually not productive, and in some cases is a formula for disaster.

Below is a sample section of a client intake policies and procedures document that focuses on the type of cases to be considered.

Client Intake Policies and Procedures

Part I: The Firm's Areas of Practice

The law firm recognizes that it can provide value to its clients by concentrating in the practice areas of land use and real estate litigation. The firm accepts clients with issues in the following practice areas:

◆ Real estate litigation
◆ Environmental matters
◆ Real estate development
◆ Zoning and planning board proceedings and appeals
◆ State agency permitting and procedures
◆ Tax abatement applications and appeals
◆ Eminent domain matters and regulatory takings

Matters not related to the above practice areas will not be accepted without the specific approval of the managing partner.

continued

It is better for a lawyer to refer a client out to another lawyer rather than to attempt to practice in an unfamiliar area. By making the referral, the lawyer is not only serving the interests of the client, but is also taking important steps in developing a referral relationship with another lawyer.

The following exchange is what might occur if a client arrives in a law office with a legal issue that is beyond the lawyer's expertise:

Lawyer: I would like to help you, but to be fair I have to tell you that I do not know much about divorce law and do not practice in that area. I can give you some help, though. If you would like me to, I do know a couple of very good domestic relations lawyers that I could refer you to.

Client: Oh, I would appreciate that. I didn't know who to turn to. You were the only lawyer I knew.

Lawyer: I am glad you came in to see me. I want you to know that if you ever come in with a problem I can't handle I will always be sure you find someone who can help. In this matter I would recommend either Attorney Smith or Attorney Jackson. I always tell clients that they have to make the decision. You may want to meet with each of them. They are both good lawyers, but it is important that you be sure you are comfortable with the one you choose.

Client: I really appreciate your help.

Lawyer: Would you like me to call them and let them know you might be calling?

Client: Yeah, that would make me feel more comfortable.

Lawyer: I will call this afternoon. And, thanks for coming in to see me. I hope you will come back if you have any other problems or questions I might help with.

When declining work, always keep marketing and public relations in mind and do your best to make the potential client comfortable with the decision to visit the firm.

Step 2: Get It Right at the Initial Client Meeting

The standard topics to be covered at an initial client meeting should be part of a law firm's policies.

- ◆ Develop a checklist of matters to be covered in the first client meeting to assure that all lawyers in the firm conduct meaningful discussions with clients about objectives, risks, the plan for going forward, and the cost.
- ◆ Make sure all lawyers in the firm provide clients with realistic expectations about legal fees, including the need for timely payments. Regardless of the clarity of the fee agreement, it is the intake discussion that will have the greatest impact on clients.

◆ If covering all the items on the checklist in one meeting is unrealistic or too ambitious, have a second meeting so that all of the checklist requirements of an initial meeting are met before significant work on the project begins.

Client Intake Policies and Procedures
(continued)

Part II: Initial Client Meeting

It is the policy of the firm to cover the following subject matters during the initial client meeting:

◆ Make sure there are no conflicts
◆ Listen to the client's story
◆ Relate back to the client the significant parts of the story
◆ Determine with specificity the client's objective
◆ Evaluate both the case and the client and decide whether the firm should take on the matter
◆ If the firm is accepting the case, describe to the client the law that applies to the problem
◆ Share with the client the matter plan or case plan
◆ Identify additional needed information
◆ Establish the method of charging legal fees and provide client with the amount of the fee or a realistic estimate

continued

Here is how that initial client conference might end:

Lawyer: Well, I hope that gives you a good understanding of the legal process you and I will be involved with and the range of possible results.

Client: Yes, I believe it does. I think I understand our chances of success and the risks we face in proceeding as you have outlined. I really appreciate you taking the time to give me such a complete understanding of what I am involved with here.

Lawyer: A good understanding at the beginning is critical in a situation such as this. Now, we also discussed that this work will be billed on an hourly basis. I gave you a preliminary case plan that included an estimate of fees. Do you have any questions about that?

Client: No, I think that is pretty clear.

Lawyer: You know I can't guarantee we will win the case, but the one thing I will promise you is that you will never be surprised by a bill I send you. If anything unexpected happens that makes it impossible for me to live with this estimate I have given you, I'll pick up the phone and give you a call and we will decide together how to address the change. That's always better than me just making decisions and you getting surprised by the amount of the fee.

Client: I agree. Sounds like I'm going to be able to sleep nights.

Lawyer: And, the one other thing I will ask of you is that if you ever get in a spot where you have trouble paying the legal fee when due, will you give me a call so we can talk about it? There are a couple of things we can do. For example, in a situation like that, clients can put the charges on a major credit card.

Client: You mean I can get frequent flier miles for my legal fees?

Lawyer: Hmmm. Yes, I guess you can. The other possibility is for us to meet again and review the relationship, because if things change and you are having trouble with the fees we might want to reconsider our plan for going forward or our fee agreement.

Client: That sounds fair to me.

This is an example of a candid discussion about fees. It puts out on the table some important contingencies. The lawyer agrees to call the client if there is a change looming that would affect the amount of the fee. This assures the client will never be surprised by the amount of a bill. In return, the client agrees to contact the lawyer if there is ever a problem paying the fee when it is due.

Step 3: Obtain a Fee Agreement and Fee Deposit

The lawyer will never be in as strong a position with the client as during that initial client meeting. This meeting is the lawyer's opportunity to have a clear and candid discussion about the costs involved in pursuing the matter.

The request for a fee deposit serves two separate purposes. It is held in a trust account and secures the prompt payment of fees when the lawyer's bill is rendered. But more importantly, any reluctance by the client to advance a fee deposit is important information. It is a clear warning sign.

Fee deposits are critical with new clients who you have not served in the past. For some clients, replenishing fee deposits is important as well. However, for existing or returning clients, it is often necessary and reasonable to waive the fee deposit requirement. That becomes a judgment call.

Consider incorporating the following into the firm's policies and procedures:

◆ Develop a set of standard fee agreements for each billing method used and have them as electronic forms that can be adapted to include the specifics of any matter.

◆ Require a signed fee agreement before commencing the work.

◆ Make certain the written fee agreement includes clear language about the requirement of timely payments and the consequences for failing to pay.

◆ Establish the amount of fee deposits for each type of work and allow exceptions only in those situations where it is clearly appropriate, based on an ongoing client relationship or the stature of the potential client.

The firm's policies and procedures involving fee agreements and fee deposits should become part of the client intake policies and procedures. For example:

Client Intake Policies and Procedures
(continued)

Part III: Fee Agreements and Fee Deposits

It is the policy of the law firm to have a written fee agreement for every matter and for all new clients, a fee deposit.

◆ A fee agreement shall be executed with regard to every matter prior to beginning the work.

◆ For every new client, the lawyer shall get from the client an initial fee deposit (to be set based on the magnitude of the work to follow, but in no event less than $2,500) prior to commencing the work.

◆ The fee agreement will clearly designate whether the fee deposit is to be held until the end of the process or, alternatively, utilized for payment of the ongoing periodic statements and to be replenished when exhausted.

◆ Exceptions to the fee deposit requirement may be made, with the approval of the managing partner, for existing clients or potential clients for whom it is deemed not necessary or not attainable.

continued

Here is how the fee deposit discussion might go:

Lawyer: Our firm policy requires me to get from you a fee deposit In the amount of $2,500 before we begin work.

Client: $2,500?

Lawyer: Yes, that is what we will need to get started. We will put it in our trust account and when we send out our monthly bills, we will deduct the amount due from that account. And, it will be what we call a replenishable fee deposit. When the amount of the remaining fee deposit drops below $500 we will ask you to replenish it with another $2,500.

Client: I don't know how I can do that. My wife has been sick and the medical bills have pretty much drained us dry. Hmmmm. . . . I am sure I could pay you . . . ah . . . sometime . . . [a long silence]. . . . Could you consider taking the case on some type of contingency?

Lawyer: No; I'm sorry, that just won't work for this case. However, I would think you might want to consult other lawyers to see if you can find one that can meet your needs in that regard.

Client: I guess I better do that. You know, we are just not the type of people who have extra money sitting around for lawyers. . . .

The potential client departs. The lawyer is reminded how important a fee deposit is in sorting out clients. The meeting was successful. The lawyer has avoided a collection problem and can now devote a full effort to paying clients. Without that fee deposit requirement, the client would have signed up and become "slow pay" at best, but more likely a complete write-off.

Step 4: The Reality Check

The client needs to be fully apprised of all the ramifications of going forward with a legal matter. The lawyer's goal is to be sure the client's enthusiasm for proceeding hasn't masked some harsh realities involved in going forward.

◆ Have a heart-to-heart discussion to determine if the client is prepared for and comfortable with the realities of the anticipated legal action and the financial commitment involved in going forward.

◆ Too many lawyers make the mistake of underplaying the cost so as to not scare off the client. Avoid that temptation.

Make the reality check a part of the client intake policies and procedure.

Client Intake Policies and Procedures
(continued)

Part IV: The Reality Check

The client must appreciate the difficulties and the costs of going forward.

- ◆ Have a discussion with the client at the end of the initial client meeting to be sure the client is prepared for what is to follow.
- ◆ Make a point of discussing the potential difficulties of the case and the burdens it will place on the client's life.
- ◆ Be sure the client appreciates the costs involved and is prepared to pay for your services.

continued

A client reality check might go something like this:

Lawyer: I just want to be sure you are prepared for what many people consider a difficult process. If you do file suit against your neighbor it is going to be an uncomfortable place to live during the litigation, which may take two or three years. Do you appreciate that?

Client: Yes, I think I understand. With him as a neighbor it is not very comfortable right now.

Lawyer: And, you realize there will be depositions and discovery requests. You will need to do quite a bit of work getting all of the documents located and organized for me. We are looking at costs in the $20,000 range. Are you sure it is worth that to you?

Client: I really think it is worth it to me, but you raise some good points. Let me sleep on it tonight and I will call you in the morning.

Most clients elect to go forward, but the extra emphasis on the problems and the costs better prepare the client for what is to come. The goal here is to be sure the client has realistic expectations with regard to the entire process.

Step 5: Confirm Client Expectations

There is always a question of how much a client hears and retains following the initial client meeting. It is always good practice to write a confirmation letter clearly setting forth the critical aspects of the initial discussion in order to reinforce the expectations that you are trying to manage.

- ♦ Following the initial meeting, confirm as much of the discussion as possible in writing so that there is no misunderstanding as to the expectations that the client should have at the outset.
- ♦ The written confirmation should include aspects of the discussion including risks and expectations that are not appropriate to include in the fee agreement. Any such information needs to be presented in a balanced and candid way.

Client Intake Policies and Procedures
(continued)

Part V: Confirming the Plans

The lawyer is responsible for completing the documentation of the arrangement.

- ♦ A signed copy of the fee agreement should go to the client and a second copy to the file.
- ♦ The lawyer should acknowledge in writing the receipt of any fee deposit and the fact that it is being held in the firm's trust account.
- ♦ The lawyer should send a letter covering any additional aspects of the representation that are not covered in the fee agreement. The letter should be used to further manage the client's expectations.

The letter might go like this:

Dear Client:

I enjoyed the opportunity to meet with you last week to discuss your legal issues pertaining to the possible right-of-way across your neighbor's property. I am pleased that you have asked us to help you with the problem.

I am enclosing a copy of the executed fee agreement for your file. I have also placed the $2,500 fee deposit in our trust account where it will be kept until we submit statements for our services. Those funds will be used to pay ongoing statements, and when the fee deposit drops below $500, we will ask you to replenish it.

I am also enclosing a copy of the case plan that we discussed. I know that you appreciate this, but I just want to say again that you may find this litigation uncomfortable. It is never easy to be involved in a lawsuit against a neighbor. I am certain there will be tension in the neighborhood during this litigation, which may go on for two or three years.

As I indicated, the result of the litigation is in doubt, but based on what I have seen so far it does appear that you have a good faith argument that you have a right-of-way across their property.

We will look forward to working with you, and we will do our best to advance your position in this litigation. If you have any lingering questions about any of this, please give me a call.

Very truly yours,

Lawyer

The key to avoiding many client problems is to recognize the significance of the client intake as the most critical meeting you have with the client. Any problems resulting from misunderstandings at that first meeting may not surface until much later in the process. Often they emerge as collection issues at or near the end of the matter. A complete client intake policies and procedure document insures a better start with a client and provides procedural guidance in managing the client's expectations (see Appendix E). Client intake is only the first step, but it establishes critical aspects of the client relationship that affect firm revenue and profits.

Offer Value-Based Fee Agreements | **10**

From the client's perspective, a fair fee is often described as being predictable and providing a value commensurate with the dollars spent. From the lawyer's perspective, a fair fee rewards the lawyer's efficiency and expertise, and provides a return on the lawyer's investment in technology and related systems. The best fee agreements are based on methods that are perceived as fair by both the client and the lawyer.

Fortunately, there are value-based fee methods that work in the best interests of both the lawyer and the client. In most circumstances, hourly billing does not meet that objective. Hourly billing does not have the effect of encouraging the lawyer to work at becoming more efficient and cost-sensitive. The client takes all the risk for any inefficiencies and the lawyer is not compelled to think about how to perform the services for the lowest possible cost. The beauty of value-based billing is that it imposes on the lawyer the need to improve practice methods to become efficient and profitable. By shifting away from hourly billing, the lawyer becomes more interested in producing the services efficiently, and both the client and the lawyer can benefit.

Lawyers need to think in terms of the value of the services they provide and create some value-based billing methods that are attractive to clients and will, in fact, better serve their own interests.

There is no single billing method that is suitable for all types of work. In fact, most lawyers recognize that hourly rate billing is here to stay, at least for some types of cases. However, lawyers need to evaluate the wide range of alternative billing methods. It is particularly useful for lawyers to be able to offer clients a choice of billing methods for any given matter.

There are a series of steps that a lawyer should take in evaluating the possibility of offering a client value-based billing.

Step 1: Know the Rules

Take a look at Rule 1.5 of the ABA Model Rules of Professional Responsibility. The first thing to notice is how many different factors may be considered in setting a fee. It raises a question as to how the profession moved so far from the Rule 1.5 standard during the last half of the twentieth century. In any event, regardless of how the profession got here, start by becoming familiar with the allowable factors:

- Time, Labor, Novelty, and Difficulty
- Likelihood of Preclusion of Other Employment
- Custom
- Amount Involved and Result Obtained
- Time Limitation Imposed
- Nature and Length of Relationship
- Experience, Reputation and Ability
- Whether Contingent or Fixed

(See Appendix F for the entire Rule 1.5.)

While knowing the factors set out in the Model Rule is a good start, be sure to examine carefully the local rules as they may differ from state to state.

Step 2: Learn Some History

Hourly billing is a fairly recent invention of legal consultants. About forty years ago consultants began preaching about the advantages of keeping track of time and using that as the basis of billing clients. For centuries before, lawyers had managed to bill clients based on a mix of factors.

While many of the billing techniques of the 1950s are not suitable in today's marketplace, the concept of value-based billing has strong roots in our profession. Find a lawyer with white hair and ask some questions about billing experiences in the early days of his or her career. And do it soon—lawyers who remember those days are getting harder to find with each passing year.

Step 3: Understand the Components to a Fair Fee

In examining and considering fee methods, always focus on the basic components of a fair fee. A fair fee:

◆ Reflects the clients perception of the value of the services
◆ Offers the client predictability of the cost
◆ Rewards the lawyer for expertise, productivity, and efficiency
◆ Provides the lawyer a return on the investment in technology
◆ Where appropriate, includes a sharing of risk

Step 4: Consider the Three Basic Alternative Billing Methods

There are three basic fee methods, in addition to the hourly billing method.

The Fixed Fee Method

Under a fixed fee arrangement, the lawyer agrees to perform certain work for a stated fee. The lawyer needs to understand the nature and extent of the work to be performed and clearly document the scope of the work in the fee agreement. Any changes or extension of the work beyond what is described becomes the subject of another agreement, or perhaps a change order (to borrow a term from the construction industry). The most critical factor is to be sure that the agreement is well documented and that there is no misunderstanding about the scope of the work to be performed for the fee, and what type of other work would require an additional fee.

Fixed fees are best used for any matter for which the lawyer can project the amount of work with some accuracy. For obvious reasons, the lawyer who specializes in a practice area is better equipped to be successful in quoting fixed fees for the range of services in that area.

Examples of work that can be performed for a fixed fee include

◆ Preparation of a will or trust
◆ Preparation of a deed or mortgage
◆ Formation of a corporation
◆ Preparation of an employee benefit plan
◆ Obtaining real estate permits and approvals
◆ Handling a DWI defense
◆ Handling a tax abatement case
◆ Handling a divorce
◆ Handling a criminal case

All lawyers can quote fixed fees for simple matters. It's the more experienced and specialized lawyer that is in the best position to quote fixed fees for a broad range of more complicated services. While it can be problematic to quote fixed fees for certain types of complicated litigation, there are ways of identifying and describing a range of predictable services to be included for the fixed fee, as well as to identify the additional services that would be considered to be beyond the basic service and therefore be charged for separately.

The fixed fee concept provides the client with a fee that is both predictable and linked to the value of the services as perceived by the client. The fixed fee can benefit the lawyer as well. While setting the fee requires skill and includes risk, it allows an opportunity for the lawyer to profit from efficiency and expertise brought to bear on the issue, an aspect that is mostly missing with hourly billing.

Sample Fixed Fee Provision

The fee for the scope of services described in the above paragraph will be at the fixed amount of three thousand five hundred dollars ($3,500.00). Any services requested that are beyond the described services will be subject to a separate fee agreement or separate charges. The fee shall be payable on or before April 1, 2005, and will not be refundable once a significant portion of the work has been performed.

[Note: this provision in intended to accurately describe a fixed fee arrangement, but please make certain it complies with your own state rules of ethics.]

Contingency Method

In a contingency fee, the lawyer's fee is determined as a percentage of the amount recovered. This is a pure form of value billing, in which the lawyer takes the risk. It is traditionally offered to clients in personal injury cases, but it can be used in any matter involving the recovery of money or with a result that can be translated to money.

Examples of work that can be performed for a contingent fee include

◆ Personal injury cases
◆ Business litigation
◆ Collections
◆ Subrogation claims
◆ Land-use matters

Personal Injury Contingency Provision

You have agreed to pay a fee contingent on the outcome of the matter. If recovery is made on your behalf, you will pay the firm the sum equal to one-third (33.3%) of any and all sums recovered by way of settlement or verdict. If any appeal to the State Supreme Court is taken, the contingent amount will increase to forty percent (40%).

If there is no recovery, you will not owe the firm any fee for representing you, but regardless of recovery, you will be responsible for all disbursements, charges and expenses incurred for . . .

[Note: this provision in intended to accurately describe the operative provision of a contingency fee arrangement, but please make certain it complies with your own state rules of ethics. For, example, some states require the client be offered the choice of an hourly rate.]

Land Use Contingency Provision

The fee for the scope of services described above will be contingent based upon the number of units approved by the Planning Board and the fee will be determined by multiplying the number of units approved by the agreed fee of nine hundred fifty dollars ($950.00) for each such approved unit.

[Note: this provision in intended to accurately describe the operative provision of a contingency arrangement, but please make certain it complies with your own state rules of ethics.]

Retainer Fee

The retainer fee is a set charge for a range of legal services over a particular period of time (and not to be confused with a fee deposit that is sometimes referred to as a retainer). For example, the client pays $1,000 per month for general advice and consultation. The services to be rendered for the retainer fee are clearly identified, so both the lawyer and client understand what is covered and what is considered extraordinary and to be billed separately.

Examples of retainer work include

♦ Business advice
♦ Municipal representation

Retainer Provision for Business Advice

For a retainer of five thousand dollars ($5,000.00), the firm will provide general corporate advice through telephone contact for the calendar year of 2005 and will assist with the annual meeting and related corporate filings, as well as preparing minutes of meetings. Any services requested that require work beyond telephone advice and the described services will be subject to a separate fee agreement or separate charges.

[Note: this provision in intended to accurately describe the operative provision of a retainer arrangement, but please make certain it complies with your own state rules of ethics.]

The value of the advice obtained by the client may exceed the retainer charges set. However, many lawyers use retainers to keep a relationship with a client and be positioned to take on the additional legal work for the client that does not fall within the routine work described by the retainer agreement.

Step 5: Consider Variations of the Basic Methods

There are a variety of innovative approaches that are variations on the three basic methods.

Blended Hourly Rates

The blended hourly rate provides that all work will be performed at a single hourly rate regardless of whether it is to be performed by a partner, an associate, or a paralegal. This method gives the client a lower blended rate (which helps avoid sticker shock) and provides the lawyer with the incentive to have as much work as possible performed by the associate or the paralegal.

Blended Rate Provision

The work performed by the lawyers and paralegals identified above will be performed at the rate of one hundred thirty-five dollars ($135.00) an hour.

[Note: this provision in intended to accurately describe the operative provision of a blended hourly rate arrangement, but please make certain it complies with your own state rules of ethics.]

Hourly Rate with Minimum and Maximum Charge

Another approach to hourly billing is to use hourly rates with a minimum and maximum charge. Fees are computed on an hourly basis with an agreement about the maximum and the minimum that will be charged. The maximum and minimum can also be adjusted, based on the result.

Hourly Rate Provision with Minimum and Maximum

I will be responsible for all work on this project and will bill my time at two hundred dollars ($200.00) per hour. However, this hourly rate agreement will be subject to a minimum fee of no less than two thousand dollars ($2,000.00) and a maximum fee of no more than four thousand dollars ($4,000.00).

[Note: this provision in intended to accurately describe the operative provision of a minimum/maximum hourly arrangement, but please make certain it complies with your own state rules of ethics.]

Budgeted Hourly Fees

The budgeting of hourly legal fees is another variation that has emerged in recent years. For example, a lawyer provides a client with a budget estimate for each of the following phases of the litigation:

- ◆ Investigation and Evaluation
- ◆ Discovery
- ◆ Final trial preparation
- ◆ Trial

Statements based on hourly rates are submitted, along with an estimate of the percentage of the work completed in each phase. The client pays based on hours worked up to the budget amount of each phase. Any billing in excess of the budgeted amount is placed in a "suspense account" to be reviewed at the conclusion of the case. If there is a good result or a valid explanation of the overrun, the client pays the excess. If not, the excess is not paid.

Segmented Fixed Fee

There are also some variations to the straight fixed-fee billing method. The segmented fixed fee is used for matters where the lawyer can predict the cost of certain components of the work, but cannot predict the course of the project from start to finish. Under the segmented fixed-fee approach, each stage of the project or each function is performed for a certain charge.

The Defense Contingency

Under this method, the lawyer and client assess the potential exposure of the case. They determine what dollar number would represent a fair result. If the lawyer is able to resolve the matter for less than the amount set, the lawyer profits by sharing in the savings. If the matter is resolved for more than the amount set, the lawyer shares in the shortfall by accepting a reduced fee.

Step 6: Consider Combination Fee Methods

Combination fee methods are useful in many routine situations where the client cannot afford a straight hourly fee and the lawyer cannot take the full risk of a contingency arrangement. These combinations allow for a middle ground with the lawyer achieving some level of cash flow while sharing the risk and reward with the client. There is a fair amount of legal work that fits in this category that otherwise might go unserviced.

Combination Flat Fee and Contingency

The lawyer charges a flat fee, to be paid in monthly installments, plus a percentage of the amount recovered. For example, the fee arrangement could be a flat fee of $12,000, payable in twelve monthly installments, plus 25 percent of the amount recovered.

Provision for Combination Flat Fee and Contingency

The legal fees will be based on a combination of a flat fee of eight thousand four hundred dollars ($8,400.00) plus a contingency based on result, as described below:

(1) The flat fee of $8,400.00 shall be paid in equal quarterly payments of two thousand one hundred dollars ($2,100.00) starting July 1, 2005, and

(2) In addition to the flat fee, the contingency fee will be fifty percent (50%) of the tax savings achieved for one year, either by settlement or court award.

[Note: this provision in intended to accurately describe the operative provision of a combination flat fee and contingency arrangement, but please make certain it complies with your own state rules of ethics.]

Combination Discounted Hourly Rate and Contingency

The lawyer charges the client monthly on a discounted hourly rate and a percentage of the amount recovered. For example, the fee arrangement could be monthly billing at the discounted hourly rate of $90 plus 20 percent of the amount recovered. With some types of cases the rate and percentage could be standard; in other matters the rate and the amount of the percentage may have to be set on a case-by-case basis.

Provision for Combination Hourly Rate and Contingency

The Combination Fee Agreement is based on reduced hourly rates plus a percentage of the amount recovered. The discounted hourly rates are one hundred twenty-five dollars ($125.00) for attorney time and seventy-five dollars ($75.00) for paralegal time. The percentage fee is twenty-five percent (25%) of the amount recovered, whether by settlement or award. We will submit statements for hourly charges on a monthly basis and request payment within thirty (30) days. The twenty-five percent (25%) of the amount recovered will be paid from the proceeds at the conclusion of the case.

[Note: this provision in intended to accurately describe the operative provision of a combination hourly rate and contingency arrangement, but please make certain it complies with your own state rules of ethics.]

Combination Hourly Fee and Flat Fee

Another possibility is a fee agreement under which the initial portion of the work is performed at an hourly rate with the balance of the work performed for a fixed fee. The lawyer charges by the hour for exploring what the client needs. Once a determination of the scope of work has been made, the lawyer can charge the balance of the work for a fixed fee.

Provision for Combination Hourly and Flat Fee

The legal fees for reviewing your assets, providing advice, and making estate planning recommendations will be at an hourly rate of two hundred dollars ($200.00). Once we agree on the estate-planning documents to be prepared and executed, the fees for those documents will be based on a flat fee for each as set out on the attached list.

[Note: this provision in intended to accurately describe the operative provision of a combination hourly and flat fee arrangement, but please make certain it complies with your own state rules of ethics.]

These combination fees provide the lawyer with some cash flow and a sharing of the risks and rewards with the client. From the client's perspective, they offer a better value and a level of predictability that is not available in hourly billing.

Step 7: Find Opportunities to Move Away from Hourly Billing

Identifying an appropriate alternative billing method is only the first step. The method must then be approved by the firm's administrator. Keep in mind that the budget is tied to the need for every lawyer and paralegal to recover their hourly rate. Also, the administrator needs a predictable monthly cash flow. These are legitimate concerns that must be recognized if the firm is to remain financially healthy.

The next hurdle is the client. While the hourly method is considered troublesome by many clients, it does have the advantage of being easy to understand: hours times rate equals the amount of the bill. Clients will be receptive to change, however, if they understand the method and have confidence in the lawyer.

Regardless of the method, the lawyer must be certain that there is a link between the value to the client and the fee charged. The lawyer is dealing with both actual value and perceived value. The communication of value becomes critical. The client who feels that he or she has received value will be receptive to an appropriate fee regardless of the method.

Having all of these concerns in mind, there are a number of steps the lawyer can take in an effort to change from hourly billing to alternative methods of billing.

Identify Repetitious Document Preparation

The drafting of documents provides an excellent opportunity for billing a flat fee (sometimes referred to as a documentation charge). Most document forms have been developed by the lawyer based on years of specialized work. With recent technological advances, the documents can be modified to fit the circumstances and printed out with a minimum of time and effort. Lawyers billing document work by the hour are giving away their expertise and probably failing to recover their technology costs as well.

This is probably the easiest area for the lawyer to depart from hourly rate billing. The lawyer's charge is appropriately based on the legal expertise brought to the problem, market conditions, and the value of the document to the client.

Understand the Cost of Providing the Service

Lawyers wanting to depart from hourly billing are in a position of having to determine an appropriate fee for entire projects. In order to quote these fees, the lawyer should review similar cases that have been completed to determine the historical amount of the total fee. If there is a pattern, it provides a basis upon which the lawyer can quote a flat fee in the new case.

A review of completed cases allows the lawyer to evaluate the staffing decisions and the efficiency with which the case was handled. Can the new case be handled more efficiently by staffing it differently? How would any such change affect the cost? Can efficiencies be brought to the case that could result in a lower charge to the client, higher profits to the lawyer, or both?

Identify Small Projects That Can Be Handled for a Fixed Fee

Moving beyond document preparation, the next step is for the lawyer to examine small projects that are reasonably predictable. Examples include tax abatement cases, administrative hearings, uncontested probate matters, loan workouts, and other matters with limited issues. Lawyers should be able to set fees in cases of this type without creating an unreasonable risk for the firm. Experiment and learn from the small matters. If the experiment works, proceed to the larger matters.

Practice Mapping Out a Case Plan at the Outset

To set a fixed fee or engage in other alternative billing methods, the lawyer needs to understand and predict the course of the case or matter, start to finish. The lawyer should map out a case plan which considers all phases of the project, including what should be done, who should do it, and what an appropriate fee to the client should be for each phase. The lawyer should go through this exercise on all cases, even those being handled on an hourly basis. It is only through practice that the lawyer will develop the habits and gain the knowledge necessary to engage in alternative billing methods. (See Appendices G-1, G-2, and G-3 for worksheets to assist in implementing value-based billing.)

Step 8: Offer Clients a Choice of Billing Methods

Give the client a choice between a straight hourly rate and a value-based fee method. Look for opportunities to share the risks and rewards. Clients appreciate a lawyer who shares the risk. In that circumstance, most clients are more than happy to share the rewards of success.

There are some large corporate clients who are wedded to hourly billing, for better or worse. However, most other clients who are offered a choice between hourly rate billing and a fixed fee will invariably choose the fixed fee. This is true even when the lawyer quotes a high fixed fee to have a cushion for the unexpected. Clients like the certainty of a fixed fee.

Most of these alternative value-based fee methods have several factors in common. They provide economic incentives for the lawyer to reduce the cost to the client and, in some cases, they call for the lawyer to share the risk with the client. They also tend to give the client more predictability as to fees. Finally, and perhaps most importantly, they attempt to base the legal fees on value provided to the client.

Shifting your billing methods to include more alternative billing should improve revenue flow. The predictability of a fee that is directly attached to the value of the services received eliminates many client issues. But more importantly, most of these alternative methods reward the knowledgeable, efficient, and productive lawyers far better than hourly billing has in recent years. Alternative billing can be beneficial to all concerned if implemented in an appropriate way.

The methods presented here are representative and not exhaustive. An excellent recent book for exploring all of the issues involved in evaluating and implementing alternative billing methods is *Winning Alternatives to the Billable Hour: Strategies That Work, Second Edition*, by James A. Calloway and Mark A. Robertson, published by the American Bar Association Law Practice Management Section.

So, What About Hours and Rates? | **11**

Remember the good old days? Law firms set hourly rates based on the partners' decisions on how much money they wanted to make the following year. That was a classic sellers' market. Law firms had a free hand in setting rates, which made budgeting a relatively simple task. So much for nostalgia; those days are gone forever.

When tightening competition put the brakes on unchecked rate increases, law firms began to increase the number of billable hours expected from each lawyer. Ratcheting up the billable-hour requirement worked for a while, but that approach got in trouble as well. Thankfully, lawyers began to see that lifestyle considerations were relevant to a healthy profession.

The lesson to be taken is that in today's world, hours and rates cannot be simply manipulated to achieve an improved revenue flow. Now, that does not mean hours and rates are unimportant. They are at the foundation of a law firm's economic model. The trick, however, is to manage hours and rates in ways that do not damage client relations or lawyer morale. The goal is to have both an acceptable revenue flow and a healthy law firm environment.

Billable Hours

At the heart of the hours issue is the question of time management and lawyer efficiency. Give some thought to the concept of the billable hour ratio—that is, the ratio of billable hours to total hours in the office.

Assume that Lawyer A and Lawyer B charge $200 an hour and have similar practices and a near-equal amount of administrative duties within the firm:

	Lawyer A	Lawyer B
Average Hours in Office per Day	9.6	8.5
Average Daily Billable Hours	4.8	7.0
Nonbillable Hours per Day	4.8	1.5

Both lawyers are spending a similar amount of time in the office. However, the ratio of billable hours for Lawyer A is 50 percent, while the ratio of billable hours for Lawyer B is 82 percent. As a result of the stronger ratio, Lawyer B is recording about 1,600 billable hours a year. Lawyer A will fall short of 1,100 hours and the revenue production difference between the lawyers based on hours will be in the order of $100,000.

Assuming Lawyer A has not taken on significant law firm administrative duties, the 50-percent billable hour ratio by all accounts would be deemed unacceptable. There are a number of possible explanations. For example, it could be that Lawyer A

- has an unacceptable work ethic;
- has insufficient work;
- does a poor job of recording time;
- writes off time before writing it down on the timesheet; or
- is inefficient or ineffective in practice methods.

Is the 50-percent ratio an extreme case? Perhaps. But most firms find that with many lawyers there is substantial room for improvement, which of course leads to better revenue flow. It does not take a time clock to judge approximate average hours in the office and compare that number to average billable hours.

The key here is to understand that more billable hours can be achieved without increasing the number of hours in the office. Too often, lawyers make the mistake of thinking that a challenge based on the number of a lawyer's billable hours leads to pressure to spend more time in the office. In fact, that is not the case. In most circumstances, it means working smarter, not harder.

Any firm that seeks to produce revenue by imposing billable hour requirements that exceed the comfort level of the partners is headed for trouble. However, if improvement in time management, office efficiency, or practice methods can increase the number of productive hours, revenues can be increased without a negative impact on the lifestyles of the lawyers and paralegals.

The goal of the firm should be to maximize the billable hours in a manner that is consistent with the culture of the firm and the revenue needs of the firm's budget. The solution focuses on aspects of personal habits, adequate staffing, appropriate delegation, work product retention, and time recording practices. To maximize billable hours, take the steps listed below.

Step 1: Determine Appropriate Billable Hour Expectations

The first step is to determine an appropriate expectation of billable hours for the partners, associates, and paralegals. There will always be a balancing between the compensation needs of the partners and the culture they are trying to create for the firm. The partners with high compensation expectations should be in firms that have high billable hour expectations. The partners who seek the benefits of a flexible lifestyle and a relaxed culture should be in firms with more reasonable billable hour expectations. To the extent that the partners disagree on the culture, accommodations need to be made through the compensation system.

The billable hour expectations of partners, associates, and paralegals are normally set at different levels. For example, the partner number may be between 1,200 and 1,800 hours, or more, depending upon the firm. Partners have substantial marketing or management responsibilities, so they have lower billable hour expectations than associates, whose expectations may range from 1,600 to 2,000 hours (or more). The billable hour number for paralegals is often in the 1,400 to 1,600-hour range, depending on the firm. This number may vary depending upon whether the paralegal has administrative responsibilities in addition to billable work. (See Appendix H for a Sample Billable Hour Policy.)

Step 2: Make Lawyers and Paralegals Accountable

Once the billable hour expectations have been determined, be sure that all timekeepers are aware of those requirements. Going forward, each timekeeper's billable hours should be tracked on a monthly basis, and at the end of the year compared to his or her billable hour expectation.

If there is a shortfall in billable hours for any individual timekeeper, the reason for the shortfall should be determined. Does it involve an unacceptable work ethic? Does the timekeeper have insufficient work? Does the timekeeper lack appropriate support? Does the timekeeper do a poor job of recording time on a daily basis? Is the timekeeper inefficient in practice methods? Does the timekeeper spend more time than necessary on nonbillable matters? The answer to these questions will lead to the appropriate solution.

Achieving billable hour expectations should be the responsibility of each lawyer and paralegal and part of the annual evaluation or salary review. If the shortfall in billable hours is attributed to a shortage of billable work or a lack of support, the lawyer or paralegal should be responsible for raising the issue with the managing partner or the practice group leader. If the shortfall is due to the habits and methods of the timekeeper, the firm should take responsibility for working with the timekeeper to correct the problem. (See Appendix I for a Sample Time Recording Policy.)

Step 3: Adopt Clear Time Recording Policies

The place where many firms lose revenue involves the failure to record billable hours accurately and on a daily basis. In order to be certain that your firm is capturing all billable time, do the following:

◆ Make certain that all timekeepers record their billable hours and submit their time sheets on a daily basis. Delay in recording causes a loss of time. The person who records each billable event as it occurs has an accurate record of the time spent. By waiting until the end of the day, time is lost. By waiting for several days, or until the end of the week, it is possible to lose as much as half of the billable time. Significant lost revenue can be recovered by the simple step of requiring a timely recording of billable hours.

◆ Adopt a firm policy that timekeepers record all billable time and do not discount the time on the time sheet. The billing partner should be the one to make any judgments as to whether the time of an associate or paralegal should be discounted. New associates, in particular, have a tendency to discount their time as they are recording it in an effort to look good to the partner that they are working for. In many cases the partner may determine that the value delivered to the client does not require such a discount. (See Appendix J for a Variable Hourly Rate Worksheet.)

Step 4: Evaluate the Secretarial Support Available to the Lawyers and Paralegals

In order to maximize billable hours, it is necessary for the lawyers and paralegals to have sufficient support. Some firms, in a cost-cutting frenzy, may decrease staff support to a level that undermines the productivity of the firm's lawyers and paralegals. While it is true that technology allows lawyers and paralegals to produce their work with less support, there can be an unfortunate backlash if sufficient support is not available.

Many new-generation lawyers are comfortable doing all of their own keyboarding. Even the more senior lawyers have developed the ability to produce their own documents. The question remains, however, as to whether that approach is the most effective and productive in any given circumstance. A careful analysis is necessary to determine whether or not lawyers are improving their productivity through their own keyboarding, or limiting the amount of work they can produce in a given day.

With increased competition and the need to produce legal work at a reasonable cost, care must be taken to see that lawyers and paralegals are not routinely spending time performing administrative and support-oriented tasks. If lawyers or paralegals are filing, copying, or straight typing, they would not be justified at billing that work at their standard hourly rates.

The concept of delegating work to the lowest level continues to be important. While technology has allowed lawyers to be more self-sufficient in many aspects of their work, it should not be used as a means to cut staff to a point where productivity is harmed. In fact, it is possible to go out of business as a result of excessive staff cuts.

In most circumstances, if there is enough client work in the firm it is better to spend the money for additional clerical support to free up lawyer and paralegal time for additional billable work. While this can be problematic if there is limited client work in the office, an argument can be made that the support should be provided so the lawyers are freed up for marketing efforts. Some lawyers with inadequate client work make the decision to limit their support and end up never getting out of the office. This can become a vicious circle.

Step 5: Take a Look at Administrative Support

Similarly, a properly run law office should have administrative support in order to allow the lawyers and paralegals to devote the majority of their time to billable work. This means having the necessary administrative help to run the office and deal with most operational matters. If one of the lawyers is spending an undue amount of time on routine administrative matters, there is a loss of revenue. Hiring an administrative person at $25 or $35 an hour allows the lawyer to bill out at $150 or $200 an hour.

Rates

Hourly rates are the foundation of law firm budgets, and have become a significant factor in law firm revenue as a result of the predominant use of hourly rate billing. Law firms are now looking for ways to diminish the use of hourly billing in favor of alternative value-based methods, but hourly rates will continue to play a role in internal budgeting and the client work that continues to be performed on an hourly basis.

One of the chief complaints about hourly rate billing is that all hours do not have the same value. What about that one-hour closing argument to a jury by a skilled trial lawyer in a big case? Picture the lawyer turning to walk back to counsel table thinking, "What a bargain the client got; $200 for that gem of a closing argument." But the lawyer also charged $200 for that hour back in the office the week before, an hour spent rummaging thorough the slightly disorganized file attempting to pull some information together. What about the hour spent before the local planning board achieving approval for a major commercial development? Is that hour worth the same as the hour spent advising clients about an issue in a residential neighborhood?

To the extent that lawyers continue to bill matters by the hour, there are some actions they can take that may improve revenue flow without simply raising rates and perhaps outpacing the market. These approaches involve recognizing that a lawyer's expertise in some areas of the practice may command higher rates than in other areas.

The Cobb Value Curve

Instructive to this discussion is the Cobb Value Curve, which first appeared in an article entitled "Competitive Pricing" in the September 1988 issue of the ABA Law Practice Management Section publication *Legal Economics.* In that article, William C. Cobb, a Houston-based law firm consultant and the principal of Cobb Consulting (WCCI, Inc.), introduced the value curve as an important planning tool for law firms.

The value curve, shown in Figure 11.1, divides legal work into four categories:

◆ Commodity: This is routine legal work that can be performed by almost any lawyer. Examples include a simple will, a deed, an uncon-

Value Curve
(Competitive Position Profile)

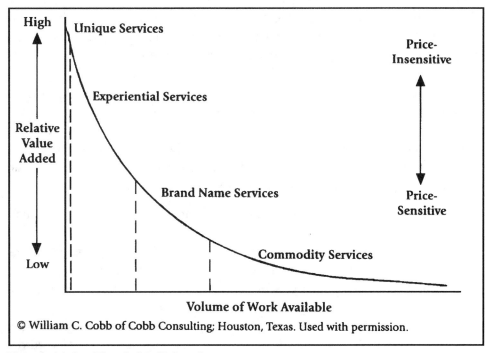

© William C. Cobb of Cobb Consulting; Houston, Texas. Used with permission.

Figure 11.1   The Cobb Value Curve

tested divorce, or a simple bankruptcy. This work is price-sensitive and clients choose their lawyers based on price. To be successful with commodity work the lawyer needs a heavily systemized volume practice.

◆ Brand Name: This is work for which the client wants a brand-name law firm. The firm is often well-known in the community, but the work may be performed by a lawyer who is less well known. Bank work, such as loan documentation, is an example. The work may be somewhat price-sensitive, but the client wants a known firm with a good reputation.

◆ Experiential: This is work for which the lawyer seeks out an individual lawyer with expertise in a particular area of the law. This work is not as price-sensitive, because there may be only one or two lawyers in the community that are the go-to lawyers for that practice specialty.

◆ Unique: This is work of a compelling nature for which cost is not a factor. It is sometimes referred to as the "nuclear wars" of the legal marketplace. It may involve a corporate takeover or an antitrust case. Only the largest firms are prepared to take on cases of this magnitude. For the client, winning is the only goal. Price is no object.

Locating the firm's work on the Cobb Value Curve can guide lawyers in many aspects of their firm management, including the cost structure, staffing, and pricing of the work. It visually supports the proposition that all hours do not have the same value. And more importantly, the value curve argues for lawyers to become more specialized and to work to become known as the go-to person in a community for a particular practice area.

Become the Go-To Lawyer

The highest rates are charged by lawyers who develop an expertise and become notable in the community as a go-to lawyer for a certain type of legal problem. While changing practice areas or developing expertise is not accomplished quickly, each lawyer needs to assess the work and look for a niche that will allow him or her to become notable in the community.

- Start by making a list of the areas of practice and types of legal matters handled.
- Give consideration to practice area lifecycles. Which practice areas are emerging as the "hot" areas for the foreseeable future?
- Conduct a market analysis to determine where the legal needs are in the community.
- Without radically changing your day-to-day practice, pick a niche area that is both on the upswing and is underserved, and work toward developing an expertise and a reputation in that practice area.

Consider Variable Rates

Not all work should be valued the same, not even when work is billed by the hour.

- Take a look at the different practice areas and types of work performed. Identify the work that is inherently more valuable, based on the knowledge and skill brought to the matter at hand, or based on the amount of money involved and the value delivered.
- Establish variable hourly rates for different types of work.

To the extent that work continues to be billed by the hour, a close look at value-related issues may logically lead to variable rates. (See Appendix J for a Variable Hourly Rate Worksheet that will assist in evaluating the possibility of variable hourly rates.)

Hours and rates can be managed to improve revenue, but an enlightened approach involves strategy and is much more complicated that simply driving the rates and the hours up, year after year, in order to meet increasing revenue demands.

Keeping Clients Thankful | **12**

Getting off to a good start with a client takes both effort and skill. The bigger challenge, however, is delivering on the expectations created and keeping clients content, day to day, during what may be difficult and stressful times. Yet it is the lawyers who are able to keep their clients thankful who earn the best rewards for the work they perform.

Surveys show that what clients want most are lawyers who care about them and their legal problems. Care and concern score as more important to most clients than the result achieved or the amount of the fee. There is a real lesson here. Treat clients as people, not files, and they will be thankful and appreciative of your efforts regardless of the difficulties that may be inherent in their legal problems. Clients who can see that their lawyers are showing concern on a regular basis are relatively content and are more likely to send their payment for fees by return mail. A client-centered service policy can lead to improved client service on a consistent basis.

Step 1: Adopt a Client-Centered Approach to the Practice of Law

A client-centered approach to the practice of law treats the needs of the client as the priority.

Client-Centered Service Policy

The firm's client-centered service policy is based on a recognition that what clients want most from their lawyers is care and concern. Often, satisfaction is based more on how the client is treated than the result obtained or the amount of the fee.

Part I: General Principles

Lawyers and staff shall endeavor to give priority to the following principles in their client relationships:

◆ Representation of a client is an interactive process
◆ The lawyer and the entire staff must develop and consistently maintain a mind-set that *it is all about the client*
◆ Clients should be treated as people, not files
◆ Responding to client contacts should be given priority
◆ Every client contact by all staff should project genuine concern for the client's issue

continued

Step 2: Set Standards for Client Communications

A client-centered approach should address both formal and informal communications with the client. The critical components of a good communication policy are given below.

◆ All staff should be instructed on the client-centered approach and given specific examples of how to interact with clients in different circumstances.
◆ Clients should be informed of the progress of their matter on a periodic basis by telephone, correspondence, fax, or e-mail. The timing of the communication should be such as is necessary to keep the client informed of the progress as a matter proceeds.
◆ The client should receive copies of all pleadings, documents, and significant correspondence as the matter progresses. If the materials are not self-explanatory, or might confuse or concern the client, the lawyer should provide an explanation of the materials.
◆ Return telephone calls and other contacts promptly. The traditional advice about returning telephone calls within twenty-four hours is totally inadequate in today's fast-paced world. If the telephone call cannot be returned within two hours, a staff member should return the call and explain to the client the extent of any further delay and find out if anyone else can help in the meantime.

- Unless other arrangements have been made, the lawyer should return all calls before the end of the day, which may mean a call in the evening. If there are reasons why it is not possible to have a substantive discussion at that time, a brief contact with an explanation will satisfy most clients.
- The lawyer should resist the temptation to delay a call to a client because some promised work has not been completed. A good client relationship needs to be based on candor and a client will be more content knowing where things stand, even if some work has not been performed as expected.
- Make sure the client is kept informed of all developments in the matter, particularly those that may adversely affect the outcome. There is nothing more harmful to an attorney-client relationship than an attorney who procrastinates in letting the client know about a troubling event. Conveying bad news must not be delayed.
- The lawyer needs to understand that a quiet client does not mean all is well. In fact, if the lawyer has not heard from a client in a while it can be a sign of a problem. Make it a habit to give a client a telephone call at least once a month even if it seems there is no reason to talk. Contact is always good, and if there is a problem the lawyer is providing an opportunity to talk about it. Look for reasons to call the client more often, not less often.

Client-Centered Service Policy
(continued)

Part II: Telephone Communications

Communications with the client should be regular and consistent with the expectations established with the client during intake. Responses to client initiated contacts should be prompt and meaningful.

- Client communication should meet the client's need and expectation.
- Clients should receive information about significant events or changes promptly.
- Communicating bad news should be a priority and should never be delayed.
- Client telephone calls should be returned within two hours, and if that is impossible, a staff member should return the call to explain the delay and find a way to get help if there is a need for immediate attention.
- Lawyers should return all calls on the same day, even if it means a return call during evening hours.

Part III: Correspondence

Written communication with the client may include traditional correspondence, faxes, or e-mail messages.

- ◆ Clients should receive copies of documents and pleadings, with a letter should the enclosure need explanation
- ◆ Clients should receive status reports monthly, unless some other arrangement has been made
- ◆ E-mail may be used for brief messages, but should not be used for confidential information or a significant communication

continued

Step 3: Use the Billing Process to Communicate Value

The lawyer's monthly bill for services is a communication tool. To benefit from the billing process, however, it is necessary to have itemized bills that convey a sense of accomplishment and value provided. Replace shortcut time entries that portray mechanical functions with more meaningful entries that reflect accomplishment and value. Take a look at the examples below that show a mechanical bill on the left and a bill reflecting the value provided on the right.

<table>
<tr><td align="center">A Bad Bill</td><td align="center">A Good Bill</td></tr>
<tr>
<td>March 4 Review file   .5 hr $100</td>
<td>March 4 Review file   .5 hr $100
materials to identify and
analyze the financial
information critical to
the agreement</td>
</tr>
<tr>
<td>March 5 Telephone   .3 hr $60
call to client</td>
<td>March 5 Telephone   .3 hr $60
call to client to
determine objectives</td>
</tr>
<tr>
<td>March 6 Research law   1.5 hr $300</td>
<td>March 6 Research legal   1.5 hr $300
implications of proposed
changes to the agreement
to see if it will be enforceable</td>
</tr>
<tr>
<td>March 7 Revise   1.0 hr $200
agreement</td>
<td>March 7 Revise agree-   1.0 hr $300
ment to include language
to insure that it will be
enforceable</td>
</tr>
</table>

March 8 Conference w/ Partner A	.5 hr	$100		March 8 Review tax partner's input on IRC s.505 on the taxability of the transaction	.5 hr	$100
Conference w/ Partner B	.5 hr	$100		Work with tax partner and revise agreement to be certain transaction will be treated as nontaxable	2.0 hr	$400
Revise agreement	1.5 hr	$300				
March 9 Finalize agreement	1.0 hr	$200		March 9 Letter to client enclosing agreement and explaining how to treat on tax return	1.2 hr	$240
Letter to client	1.2 hr	$240			**8 hrs**	**$1,600**
	8.0 hrs	**$1,600**				

It is not difficult to picture a client receiving the mechanical bill and being disturbed by the cost of the project. On the other hand, the client reading the more detailed bill can better appreciate the work that has been done for the cost.

Client-Centered Service Policy
(continued)

Part IV: Communications Through the Billing Process

The billing process is an excellent client communication tool.

◆ Time entries on itemized bills should avoid reciting mechanical functions but rather should be used to communicate substantive accomplishments and value provided.

◆ Monthly bills should be sent with a cover letter briefly summarizing the work performed and the work planned for the following month.

continued

In addition to providing a detailed bill, it is also helpful to provide a cover letter that provides an update on what has been accomplished and a projection of work anticipated for the following month. Such a letter in a litigated case might go something like this:

Dear Client:

I am enclosing our statement for services during October 2004. As you can see from the description of the work, we completed the depositions of the defendants and have successfully uncovered the repair records through court-ordered discovery. During November, we expect to have our expert examine the remains of the furnace and complete his report. He may be contacting you directly if he has any questions. Once the expert reports are exchanged, which will probably occur in early December, we will proceed to arrange the experts' depositions.

Thank you for the prompt payment of our statement last month. Should you have any questions or concerns about the enclosed statement, or any other aspect of the case, please let me know.

Very truly yours,

Lawyer

Step 4: Manage the Client's Expectation of Cost

In order to make good on any cost estimates provided, it is critical to track the progress of the case and compare it to the billing from month to month. To the extent that the client has expectations with regard to the overall fee, it is necessary to monitor the progress. If anything changes that would result in not being able to meet the estimate, then notify the client and invite further discussions as to how to proceed. The process should go something like this:

- ◆ The lawyer should have accessible a copy of any case plan or fee estimate provided each client for reference from time to time.
- ◆ All staff should be familiar with the case plan and fee estimate as everyone needs to manage the case within the parameters of the client's expectations.
- ◆ At the time of monthly billing, the lawyer should refer to the estimate and track the progress of the case.
- ◆ If the fee estimate is no longer appropriate, then the lawyer needs to either adjust the manner in which the case is being handled, or contact the client to discuss the need for an adjustment to the estimate.
- ◆ The lawyer needs to discuss with the client any changes in the overall fee prior to the client receiving a bill for services inconsistent with the original fee discussion.

Client-Centered Service Policy
(continued)

Part V: Managing Client Expectations

The client's expectations must be managed throughout the process.

- Any significant change in the course of a matter or a case plan must be shared with the client at the earliest possible time.
- The case plan and any fee estimate should be easily accessible and re-ferred to regularly during the course of a matter.
- Lawyers and staff need to be familiar with the case plan and fee esti-mate as everyone needs to cooperate in managing a case within the pa-rameters of the client's expectations.
- At the time of monthly billing, the lawyer should refer to the fee esti-mate.
- If the fee estimate cannot be met, the lawyer needs to adjust the matter in which the matter is handled or contact the client to discuss adjust-ing the amount of the estimate.
- Contact a client in advance if a monthly bill is higher than the client ex-pects, thereby being careful never to surprise a client with the amount of a bill.

continued

A letter to the client alerting a client to a developing problem with the fee estimate might look like this:

Dear Client:

Last month, the expert examined the remains of the furnace and he believes that it was not the model you thought had been installed in your home, but rather is a lesser model that could not safely perform as you had expected. In order to verify his opinion he has asked me to conduct additional depositions of several company employees. The depositions he is suggesting, and the discovery necessary in preparation, will involve three to five additional days of work, which would add approximately $5,000 to your costs.

To this point, our monthly charges to you have tracked our original estimate. However, the suggested depositions were not in the original case plan and were not included in the scope of the work leading to our fee estimate. While these depositions may not have been considered essential earlier, I do recommend them as I anticipate the information gained will strengthen our position and increase the likelihood of success.

As I indicated to you in our initial meeting, I do not want to take any action that will cause me to exceed the fee estimate without discussing the matter with you.

I will be contacting you within a few days to discuss with you how best to proceed.

Very truly yours,

Lawyer

Step 5: Recovery Issues

Although not part of a lawyer's jargon, the concept of recovery needs to be borrowed from other service-industry programs. Recovery is the means by which a problem is corrected. If a customer has a problem or has become unhappy about some aspect of the service, the best approach is to correct the situation as soon as possible and not let the unhappiness fester. Delay only makes things worse.

If the lawyer understands from a telephone message that a client is unhappy, the callback should be immediate. Lawyers must avoid the temptation to put the unhappy client's telephone message at the bottom of the pile. Similarly, never delay if there is bad news to deliver to a client. The passage of time will not make the call easier or the news better. In fact, the passage of time will make it worse. Adopt this policy:

- ◆ If the staff gets a call from a client that reflects client unhappiness, the message should be relayed to the lawyer as soon as possible.
- ◆ Upon receiving a message suggesting client unhappiness, the lawyer should return the call to the client with lightning speed. Unhappiness festers and it is essential to a good client relationship to respond promptly and work out a solution, whatever the issue.
- ◆ The lawyer should make a return call immediately, even if it will take a follow-up discussion later to actually solve the problem. A brief contact is better than delay.

Client-Centered Service Policy
(continued)

Part VI: Recovery

If a client has a problem or becomes unhappy with some aspect of the service, the situation should be addressed as soon as possible so that the matter will not fester.

◆ If a client calls and leaves a message expressing unhappiness with some aspect of the service, the return of the phone call must have the highest priority.

◆ Staff members who are aware of a telephone message in which a client expresses unhappiness with some aspect of the service must get word of the call to the lawyer ASAP (and not simply leave the message on the lawyer's desk).

◆ Never delay returning a call to a client who has left a message expressing unhappiness with any aspect of the service.

continued

See Appendix K for a Sample Client-Centered Service Policy.

Adopt a client-centered service approach. Treat clients as people, not files. Make sure the entire staff understands *it is all about the client.* It is the satisfied clients who pay their legal bills on time, often by return mail.

Technology: Finding the Profits 13

$\mathbf{W}$hat has been the impact of technology on the practice of law? For too long, technology has been perceived as a major expense and hassle for most lawyers. Clients who have mastered technology in their businesses have required their law firms to be technologically advanced. Many firms have been forced to meet the challenge, regardless of their inclination and whether or not the necessary funds were in the budget. Other firms struggle with the need for technology and its impact on the professional lives of the lawyers and the negative effect on the firm's bottom line.

For starters, lawyers recognize that technology has improved administrative and communication functions that make the practice of law and client service more efficient and effective. These include e-mail, time and billing systems, electronic files, electronic billing, client access to electronic files, cell phones, PDAs, and so on. These capabilities are a helpful component of any law firm and an expense that needs to be accepted and worked into the budget.

But when the discussion moves to the creation of work product, a problem arises. The combination of technology and hourly billing has created a real difficulty for some lawyers. The ability to produce valuable work product more quickly works against the lawyer who continues to bill by the hour. Think about wills, trusts, purchase and sales agreements, and so on. It may take ten hours for the lawyer to draft the first such document, due to the need to research potential issues and make certain the document is adequate and covers unexpected contingencies. The second time the lawyer is asked to produce such a document it will undoubtedly take less time; assume two hours for the purposes of discussion.

Once the lawyer has produced such a document several times, it may take only a short while to meet with the client and then tailor the document to cover the specific concerns of the new client. Is the value of that work only 20 percent of the work performed for the first client? The answer is obviously no. And, in the same regard, the value of the work for the first client is not five times greater than the work done for the second client. This is a prime example of the problem with hourly billing and the need for a value-based billing method.

Misguided Lawyers

Lawyer A: Well, Mr. Smith, we will prepare the trust as we discussed. My charges will be based on a hourly rate of $200 an hour. That may sound like a lot, but we have a template of the trust on the computer so it is just a matter of pressing a button. Isn't technology wonderful?

****

Lawyer B: Well, Mr. Smith, we will prepare the trust as we discussed. Our standard charge for that trust is $2,250, but we do keep track of our time and if we can do it more quickly we won't charge you for more than the hours it actually takes to produce the document.

The examples above are situations where the charge should be based on the value of the product through the use of a flat fee. Lawyer B (based on a true story) thought he "got it" in setting a flat fee, but in fact he had the worst of both worlds. He capped the upside of his fee, but not the downside.

Utilizing technology as a profit factor does not happen naturally. The law firm needs to take the initiative to study the differing practice areas to determine how best to convert the technological capabilities into a revenue enhancer.

Addressing technology issues starts with a preliminary review of systems to be sure the firm is on a sound footing with regard to basic functions. Once the basic functions are under control, the firm can then tell whether its use of technology properly generates revenue and profits.

Step 1: Make Sure the Firm's Technology Is on Sound Footing

Let's start with some basics. Does the firm have its technology under control? Do the lawyers understand the capability of the technology and use it in their practices? Or is your firm one of the many that spends money on software programs that the lawyers do not use?

First, determine to what extent the firm is going to use technology as an administrative and communication tool. Be sure the firm has selected appropriate calendaring, communication, time and billing, and other administrative software in order to develop valuable systems for managing the lawyers and the work in the firm.

- ◆ Have a firm-wide calendaring system that lawyers are able to access from outside the office. Make a decision as to whether to provide lawyers with hand-held remote devices.
- ◆ Provide lawyers with e-mail addresses and encourage communication within the firm and with clients using e-mail. In the process, consider issues of confidentiality and obtaining clients' approval for the use of e-mail for client communication.
- ◆ Network the computers in the office and identify one as a server to be the repository for all of the firm's files. Require all lawyers to save documents to the server and not solely on their individual computers.
- ◆ Develop a uniform system within the firm for identifying and saving valuable work product to electronic form files.
- ◆ Organize electronic form files with standard letters and documents.
- ◆ Spend the money necessary to train the lawyers to operate the technology the firm has decided to use.

Step 2: Take a Look at the Firm's Document Production Practices

Most lawyers whose practices are based largely on document production have adopted value-based billing in the form of flat fees. This is the area of the practice of law that best lends itself to some variation of flat-fee billing. However, the use of flat fees is not universal and there are a large number of lawyers who continue to produce documents based on hourly billing.

- ◆ Examine the firm's transactional practice areas and determine the billing methods used for document production services.
- ◆ Start with the most simple and predictable client services that the firm performs on a repetitive basis, and either develop or organize template documents that can be adapted for each new client.
- ◆ Create a system through a written case or matter plan with sample documents and written instructions.
- ◆ Consider using computerized substantive software systems where available and suitable for your practice area.

◆ Establish a standard value-based fair fee for specific documents or transactions.

◆ Develop standard fee agreements for the service.

The goal is to be able to charge a fair and competitive fee to the client while using technology in order to increase the firm's profit margin.

Step 3: Find Places to Deliver Standard Service Packages

In Step 2 above, we looked at fairly routine and simple services where the lawyer is producing one or a few documents in a transactional situation. Document preparation can be extended to offer standard packages. The extension of the document preparation is to find somewhat more extensive services to offer is what might be called a standard package. In looking for these opportunities, it is important that the lawyer have expertise in the area and provide these services on a regular basis.

◆ Examine a broader range of services provided by the firm and identify projects or cases that are reasonably predictable in their process and course.

◆ Look for and consider computer software systems that allow the systemization of work suitable for the practice area.

◆ To the extent the project or case does not lend itself to computerized software, develop systems, forms, and written instructions.

◆ Look at and evaluate completed files in order to establish a value-based fair fee for the service package.

◆ Develop standard fee agreements for the service.

Step 4: Look for Other Places to Develop and Offer Value-Based Fee Methods

Technology costs are weighing heavily on many firms that continue to bill by the hour. It is only by moving in the direction of alternative billing methods that law firms will truly benefit from the investment of time, energy, and money in technology.

◆ Have each practice group in the firm identify services that might be offered for a value-based fee.

◆ Go slow, and never experiment with more than 15 percent to 20 percent of the firm's business at any one time.

◆ Monitor results from the value-based fee work. If it is successful, consider expanding the amount of value-based fee method work performed by the firm.

Technology can be more than an extraordinary expense and a hassle for lawyers. But to turn it into a profit factor, lawyers need to benefit from the efficiencies achieved through the increased use of value-based fee agreements.

Paralegals: Expanding the Role **14**

Where do paralegals fit in the revenue picture? Their role in the delivery of legal services has increased substantially as the associate pyramid has collapsed. Today, paralegals perform work that in the past may have been performed by associates. If their work is properly priced, paralegals can provide good profits for their firms.

Properly trained and supervised, paralegals provide solid value to law firms and their clients. However, keep in mind that it takes more than hiring a paralegal to achieve these benefits. The paralegal needs to be well qualified and have talents and skills for a particular role. Having the confidence of the lawyer and the clients is the most significant ingredient necessary for success. Look for paralegals who are career employees and who have expertise in one practice area.

Step 1: Hiring Real Paralegals

The first step is to be sure to hire real paralegals. Think about the educational requirements. While there are some good paralegals who have come up through the system, most firms now consider a bachelor's degree to be the minimum educational requirement. As the work of paralegals becomes more complex and demanding, the need for good educational background and training has become more important.

When evaluating the educational credentials of a paralegal applicant, a good source of information is the ABA Web site for paralegals (**http://www.aba net.org/legalservices/paralegals/**), which also provides a list of paralegal programs that are ABA-approved.

Beyond the educational requirements, take some time to think about the qualifications needed for the particular paralegal role to be filled. Some paralegal positions require people with good communication skills, while other positions may be for people who end up in the back room working with numbers and schedules. Some paralegals do research and analysis while others simply process routine documents. The skills required vary, depending on the practice area and the nature of the work delegated. (See Appendix L for a Sample Paralegal Hiring Policy.)

Do not overlook the question of whether the paralegal candidate is a good match for the supervising lawyer. The paralegal's level of success may be directly related to how much confidence the lawyer has in the paralegal. No other factor is more important.

When looking for a paralegal, do not fall into the trap of hiring the person with the lowest salary demand. The initial reaction of some lawyers is that well-qualified paralegals command high salaries and will not yield the profits desired. They think they can make more money with a low-paid entry-level paralegal. Nothing is further from the truth.

In most circumstances, the lawyer can justify billing an experienced paralegal at double the hourly rate of an entry-level paralegal. Even if the firm pays an experienced paralegal twice as much as the entry-level paralegal, the profits generated by the experienced paralegal will be greater. It is the overhead costs that make this so. They will be nearly the same for both paralegals. Consider the two extremes:

	Entry-level	Experienced
Salary	$30,000	$ 60,000
Fringe Benefits and Overhead Costs	$35,000	$ 40,000
Total Costs	$65,000	$100,000
Hours	1,500	1,500
Hourly Rate	x 50	x 100
Potential Revenues	$75,000	$150,000
Less 10 % Uncollectible	$ 7,500	$ 15,000
	$67,500	$135,000
Less Costs	$65,000	$100,000
Profit	$ 2,500	$ 35,000

There are firms that manage acceptable profits from entry-level paralegals by increasing their billable hour requirements. For example, the $2,500 profit shown above can be increased to $16,000 by increasing the billable hour requirement at the entry level to 1,800 hours. But, with the need for extensive training during the first six to twelve months, most entry-level paralegals cannot achieve high billable hours.

Modifications can be made to the model based on individual circumstances. However, the resulting analysis is likely to demonstrate that in most settings, larger profits are achieved by hiring or developing and retaining experienced paralegals.

And finally, be sure to recognize that the most critical aspect may be compatibility with the lawyers and the level of confidence that can be developed in the lawyer-paralegal relationship. No other factor is more important.

Step 2: Evaluate the Current Paralegals

For paralegals already employed by the firm, take a look at who they work for and what they do. Evaluate each paralegal and the relationship with each lawyer with whom he or she works, as well as the clients. Confidence is the key factor. If the lawyers or the clients do not have confidence in the paralegal, this is a signal that the paralegal will not be successful in producing maximum revenue for the firm. In those circumstances, the firm should reevaluate the situation and make the necessary changes. Firms cannot afford unproductive lawyers or unproductive paralegals.

Step 3: Evaluate the Work

What is the role of a paralegal? In many firms the role is misunderstood. And the resulting underutilization prevents those firms from achieving the desired revenue potential. In fact, any substantial underutilization (which is not all that uncommon) causes paralegals to become an unrecoverable cost as opposed to a profit component of the firm.

In 1997, the ABA defined the paralegal's role as performing substantive legal work that would otherwise be done by lawyers. By articulating the role in that way, the ABA made the point that paralegal work is much the same as lawyer work; it is not clerical or administrative work. On the other hand, paralegals cannot practice law, which means they cannot accept a case or set a fee, give legal advice, make a legal decision, chart the direction of a case, or appear in court. While it is always necessary to check any local variations to the Rules of Professional Responsibility, most other work can be performed by a paralegal provided it is under the supervision of a lawyer. (See Appendix N for Paralegal Billing Guidelines.)

- Take a look at the paralegal role in each practice area.
- Determine whether the role can be expanded under the local rules.
- If the role can be expanded, prepare policies and procedure describing the paralegal role.
- Examine the qualifications and skills of the paralegals and their suitability for their present assignments based on the skills and talents they bring to their position.
- Consider focusing paralegals in one or more practice areas in order to increase their expertise.
- Consider assigning each paralegal to an individual lawyer or, in the alternative, to a practice group. The more lawyers a paralegal works with, and the more diverse the work, the less effective and less productive the paralegal will be.

Step 4: Price the Paralegal Services

In order to achieve the optimum profits from the paralegal work, lawyers must properly price those services. It does no good to move additional work to paralegals if that work is performed at a loss. A paralegal profit study can be accomplished by analyzing costs and revenues for each paralegal or by applying a rule of thumb known as the "rule of three," a historically accepted test for determining the profitability of paralegals. If the revenues generated by the paralegal equal three times his or her salary, the test is met. The rule assumes that the first one-third represents the paralegal's salary, the second one-third represents fringe benefits and the paralegal's share of the overhead costs, and the last one-third represents profits to the lawyer. Let's take a look at how this would work:

Hourly Rate	x	Billable Hours	=	Revenue div by 3	=	Salary
$125		1,500		$187,500		$62,500
$100		1,600		$160,000		$53,333
$100		1,400		$140,000		$46,666
$ 75		1,600		$120,000		$40,000
$ 75		1,400		$105,000		$35,000
$ 60		1,600		$ 96,000		$32,000
$ 60		1,400		$ 84,000		$28,000

The rule of three is a good test for most small and midsized law firms. The rule may have suffered some erosion in recent years in large firms with high costs, where the "rule of three and a half" is probably a better test. However, keep in mind that although this rule of thumb is a good starting point, it is always better to determine the actual costs for each paralegal.

Step 5: Set Production Goals for the Paralegals

The paralegals are a revenue-producing component of the law firm. For the most part, their primary role should be working on billable services. Clerical and administrative functions should be moved to less-qualified employees. The firm should have billable hour goals for the paralegals. Provided they have sufficient support, paralegals should be billing between 1,200 and 1,600 hours each year.

Step 6: Provide Paralegals with Adequate Support

As a valuable profit-producing component of the firm who need to have significant billable hours, paralegals need a level of support. Those firms that do not provide paralegals with secretarial and administrative support make a mistake. Paralegals cannot bill for the portion of the work that is clerical or administrative. This means fairly highly paid paralegals would be using their time to perform tasks that could be performed by employees making half their salary.

In some practice areas, paralegals may produce most documents on a computer and need limited support. In other situations, a paralegal may need significant secretarial support in order to maximize the number of billable hours. However, each situation is different and the goal must be to provide whatever support is necessary to make each paralegal as productive as possible.

While some firms will continue to leverage with associates, their role will increasingly be viewed as partner trainees and their worth to the firm evaluated on that standard. Paralegals will continue to see an increasing role in supporting the partners in the delivery of legal services. (See Appendix M for a Paralegal Profitability Worksheet.) For additional information on paralegals and law firm profitability, see *Paralegals, Profitability, and the Future of Your Law Practice*, by Arthur G. Greene and Therese A. Cannon, published by the American Bar Association Law Practice Management Section.

If All Else Fails: **15**
Using the Band-Aid®

What about a collection policy? If the recommendations of this book succeed, there will be no need for a collection policy. However, it will take time before the recommendations can be realized. Also, there is always the possibility of a few clients becoming a collection problem, even under the best of circumstances. Therefore, every firm needs a collection policy.

Most firms with collection problems lack a standard policy or fail to consistently apply an existing policy. The longer an overdue receivable goes without attention, the more courage the client gains for further delay of payment. Most lawyers make the mistake of not addressing receivables until they are in the sixty-to ninety-day range. Unfortunately, at that stage the client is becoming conditioned to understanding that timely payment does not seem to be particularly important. Therefore, the best approach is for the firm's policy to address overdue receivables in quick order and with consistency.

Step 1: Adopt a Law Firm Collection Policy

For example, a collection policy might include the following:

- ◆ Any bill going to the client with a back due balance should include a letter noting that the past due balance is unacceptable and requesting immediate payment.

- The firm should have a procedure for tracking the age of receivables and notifying the attorney and the appropriate staff person when the receivable reaches a specific age. The key to a successful collection policy is for the client to know that there is a problem if the bill is not paid in thirty days. The collection process needs to kick in about thirty days following the billing date, but in no event later than forty-five days.
- There should be a telephone contact with the client no later than forty-five days following the date of the bill. If agreement cannot be reached in that first call, or if agreement is reached but payment is not made, the second call should be for the purpose of setting up a meeting with the client to reevaluate the relationship.
- The arranged meeting should be similar to the intake meeting. The attorney and client should reevaluate the objective of the work, the status of the matter, and on what basis it makes sense to go forward. The meeting could end with:
  - A payment of back due fees through the use of a credit card or other financing
  - A restructuring of the fee agreement, or a change in the objective or plan going forward due to cost considerations
  - The replenishing of the fee deposit thorough the use of a credit card
  - A termination of representation

The goal is to use the threat of the meeting to provide incentive for clients to pay before a meeting becomes necessary. If that doesn't work, then the meeting provides a basis to change the arrangement, since the client is unable to live up to the terms of the original fee agreement.

The letter with the following month's statement might say:

Dear Client:

I am enclosing our statement for services during October 2004. As you can see from the description of the work, we completed the depositions of the defendants and have successfully uncovered the repair records through court-ordered discovery. During November, we expect to have our expert examine the remains of the furnace and complete his report. He may be contacting you directly if he has any questions. Once the expert reports are exchanged, which will probably occur in early December, we will proceed to arrange the experts' depositions.

I note with concern that your last month's statement has not been paid. If payment cannot be made at this time, please give me a call to discuss the options available.

Very truly yours,

Lawyer

The letter would be followed with a phone call no more than seven days later.

Client: Hello.

Staff: Hello, this is Beverly at Attorney Brown's office. How are you today?

Client: I am doing well, thanks.

Staff: I am calling because we notice that your statement for work in October did not get paid. You had been paying each month as provided in the fee agreement, so this caught us by surprise. Is everything OK? Was there a problem with the bill?

Client: Oh . . . ah . . . no, everything is fine. It's just I have had some heavy expenses lately . . . so I just need a little time.

Staff: Back at that first meeting, did Attorney Brown tell you that we have an arrangement to accept credit cards to help our clients out in situations like this?

Client: Yes, he did mention that.

Staff: Would you like to put that charge on a credit card, or would you prefer that I set up a meeting for you with Attorney Brown to reevaluate the relationship?

Client: Can you hang on just a minute while I get my credit card?

Staff: Sure, take your time . . .

The collection policy should be designed to make it clear to the client that the failure to pay legal fees is not acceptable and that the developing payment problem must be addressed swiftly. The policy should be designed to avoid the prolonged and erratic process of collection efforts through repeated calls.

Step 2: Make the Collection Policy and Procedure a Priority

Don't let procrastination cause lawyers to avoid collection issues. It is way too easy for lawyers to decide that there are more pressing matters in serving their clients' day-to-day needs.

◆ Officially adopt a collection policy and procedure (see Appendix O for a Sample Law Firm Collection Policy).

- Train all lawyers and staff to perform their roles under the collection policy and procedure.
- Develop and implement a process for monitoring of the collection effort.
- Make work under the collection policy and procedure a priority by including it as a consideration in staff salary reviews and partner evaluations.

Step 3: Other Approaches

Develop some alternative approaches to be utilized in certain circumstances. For example:

- Where appropriate, convince clients to call in each month and put their bill on a credit card.
- If there are continuing services needed, consider the possibility of terminating your services if an acceptable arrangement cannot be achieved. It is always necessary to be sure termination of services is permitted under the fee agreement with the client and applicable rules of professional conduct.
- On very old receivables, consider making agreements to accept a discounted payment from clients for whom there are no ongoing services and little likelihood of a future attorney-client relationship.

Yes, a collection policy is essential to every firm. And it is the prompt and consistent application of such a policy that achieves results. However, do not lose sight of the goal, which is to manage clients and their expectations in a way that eliminates the need to act under the collection policy.

For additional information on the issues involved in increasing client satisfaction and the collection effort, see *Collecting Your Fee: Getting Paid from Intake to Invoice*, by Edward Poll, and *The Essential Formbook, Volume II: Human Resources/Fees, Billings, and Collection*, both books published by the American Bar Association Law Practice Management Section.

Making It Work

The remarkable part of all of this is that the financial indicators can clearly show where to make improvements. Remember, the key is *to find ways to improve revenue without increasing costs.* If that can be accomplished, it takes very little additional revenue to make a significant increase in the profits to the partners.

But wait . . . there is a glitch. The solution is not learning how to better manipulate the numbers; rather it involves being open to changing some practice methods and taking some steps to improve the lawyer-client relationship. What started out as a math problem quickly becomes a challenge to some habits and practice methods of lawyers.

Too many lawyers simply go along for the ride, letting events shape their futures. They try to do better by attracting more clients or by adding lawyers to the firm. They spin their wheels faster and faster, an experience that gives them the feeling they must be doing better, but at the same time they are avoiding the underlying issues that are limiting their success. They do not recognize that it is most likely their underlying practice methods or the nature of their existing client relationships that prevents them from attaining better revenue.

The approaches suggested in this book go to the heart of the problem—client expectations. It is the improvement of client relationships through better client-service policies and changes in practice methods that will provide the expected improvement in the financial indicators.

Taking the First Step ... and Another Step ... and then Another ...

16

Implementing the recommendations of this book cannot be achieved simply by the hard work of a managing partner or a law firm manager. Moving the law firm to a revenue mindset and implementing the changes in practice methods, fee agreements, and client-service approaches must reflect a decision of the firm and all of its lawyers. Without a strong commitment from the lawyers, the efforts are doomed to erratic application and ultimate failure.

Once the firm has lawyer buy-in, the next challenge is to develop the long-range plan to guide the firm in implementing the agreed-to changes. There may be questions about the order in which issues are addressed, and the approaches that are to be taken. While the specifics of the plan depend on the circumstances in each individual firm, the following represents a typical approach:

- Conduct a firm retreat to present the advantages of adopting a revenue mindset and employing certain new techniques and practice methods in order to improve revenue and profits.
    - The retreat would be to educate the firm's partners (or lawyers) as to how increased revenue and profits will flow from certain changes
    - To demonstrate what might be accomplished, the managing partner should complete and present to the part-

ners the firm scorecard reflecting both the firm's revenue capacity and the firm's performance for the most recent fiscal year

♦ Partner buy-in to the concepts is critical to the effort

♦ Decide which changes to make and then develop a phased approach for implementing the agreed-to changes in the order that makes sense to the firm. Each separate phase should have a timetable and a person responsible for implementation. Monthly partner meetings should be used to monitor progress and vote on the details of policies and procedures as the work on each phase is completed. For example:

  ♦ Conduct a paralegal profitability study. (one month)
  ♦ Adopt a paralegal hiring policy. (one month)
  ♦ Adopt a billable hour policy. (one month)
  ♦ Adopt a time recording policy. (one month)
  ♦ Develop and adopt a client-centered service policy. (two months)
  ♦ Develop and adopt client intake policies and procedures. (two months)
  ♦ Adopt a collection policy. (three months)
  ♦ Study, develop and adopt variable hourly rates. (six months)
  ♦ Develop and begin to adopt alternative value-based fee agreements. (six months)

♦ While some of these matters could be the subject of prolonged study and development, the goal should be to get progress on all of these initiatives within one year. Further refinement or course corrections may continue indefinitely. Understand that improvement in the financial indicators will be incremental and it will be three to five years before the firm feels it has achieved complete success.

♦ Track the financial trends from year to year through the use of the financial indicators.

  ♦ Complete the scorecard each year and establish as a goal a reasonable incremental improvement for the following year.
  ♦ Provide lawyers with meaning financial reports each month to track progress.
  ♦ Assign responsibility to the practice group leaders to work with the lawyers and paralegals to find ways to make sure the annual goals are met.

Success will depend on whether the firm's lawyers have the patience and the focus to stick with the plan and the timetable until the desired results are achieved. See Appendix P for a Planning Worksheet to guide the process.

Final Thoughts **17**

The vast majority of law firms leave *money on the table* . . . that is, there are places where revenue can be improved easily. In order to find those places, it is necessary to have in place time and billing software and financial software that has been configured to produce reports that track the financial indicators. Take the time to organize the financial indicators on a scorecard and set some goals for incrementally improving each of the indicators. Small improvements in several areas can result in large increases of revenue.

The best ways to improve the indicators is to use approaches that also improve client satisfaction and law firm morale. Fee deposits and aggressive collection policies are sometimes necessary, but the more important strategy is to provide clients with realistic expectations at the outset and manage those expectations throughout the matter. Client satisfaction is the most important ingredient to keeping the revenue flowing. All of this may take a new attitude in the firm: *It's all about the client.*

At the same time the firm is addressing client issues, it also needs to find ways to improve its practice methods and its approach to leverage. Value-based fee agreements are a key to leverage in the twenty-first century and also help with good client relations. Find ways to use technology in the delivery of those services.

There is no silver bullet that ensures improved revenue. Rather, improvement comes from paying better attention to what is important, and making a series of changes to many aspects of the firm's practice. It will take a focus on these issues, patience to

109

carry out a long-term plan, and willingness to persist until the mission is accomplished. The chapters in this book have attempted to set forth some practical step-by-step approaches to guide your firm through the process. While the process may be a bit tedious, the concepts are simple and in many cases obvious.

The remarkable part of all of this is that the firm's financial indicators will make it clear that there are places for improvement. Remember, the key is *to find ways to improve revenue without increasing costs.* If that can be accomplished, it takes very little additional revenue in order to make a significant increase in the profits to the partners.

Appendix A-1

Financial Reports

Profit and Loss Statement March 2005

	March	Year to Date	Budget to Date	Variance	%
Income					
Legal Fee Income	$98,570	$276,450	$300,000	($23,550)	92%
Other Income	75	157	—	157	—
Total	$98,645	$276,607	$300,000	($23,393)	92%
Expenses					
Advertising	$ 1,411	$ 3,500	$ 3,000	($500)	117%
Bank Service Charges	140	420	420	—	100%
Conferences and Seminars	—	—	750	750	—
Contributions	500	500	800	300	63%
Credit Card Service	250	750	750	—	100%
Dues and Subscriptions	—	200	400	200	50%
Professional Liability Insurance	1,250	3,750	3,750	—	100%
Office Expense					
Computers	450	2,345	1,500	(845)	156%
Postage and Delivery	140	476	500	24	95%
Printing and Reproduction	180	375	450	75	83%
Supplies	850	2,597	2,500	(97)	104%
Telephone	479	1,475	1,200	(275)	123%
Payroll					
Associates	10,000	30,000	30,000	—	100%
Paralegals	6,750	20,250	20,250	—	100%
Staff	6,200	18,600	18,600	—	100%
Fringe Benefits	3,375	8,850	8,200	(650)	108%
Payroll Taxes	2,070	6,210	6,210	—	100%
Library	1,238	3,330	3,200	(130)	104%
Occupancy					
Building Services	625	1,875	1,875	—	100%
Rent	2,575	7,725	7,725	—	100%
Insurance	250	750	750	—	100%
Utilities	452	1,450	1,375	(75)	105%
Professional Services	—	—	600	600	—
Total	$39,185	$115,428	$114,805	($623)	101%
Profit/Loss	$59,460	$161,179	$185,195	($22,770)	87%

Appendix A-2

Financial Reports

Billable Hours
March 2005

	MTD Goals	MTD Actual	MTD Variance	YTD Goals	YTD Actual	YTD Variance
By Individual						
Lawyer A	133	140	7	400	375	(25)
Lawyer B	133	115	(18)	400	362	(38)
Lawyer C	133	165	32	400	460	60
Paralegal A	125	132	7	375	377	2
By Practice Group						
Litigation 3 Lawyers 2 Paralegals	782	792	10	2346	2307	(39)
Business 2 Lawyers 2 Paralegals	516	496	(20)	1548	1578	(30)
Real Estate 1 Lawyer 1 Paralegal	258	279	21	774	805	31
Estate Planning and Probate 2 Lawyers 3 Paralegals	1,016	995	(21)	3048	3048	—

Appendix A-3

Financial Reports

Billing and Billing Realization March 2005

	MTD Billings	MTD Dollar Value Billings	MTD Billing Realization	YTD Billing	YTD Dollar Value Billings	YTD Billing Realization
Individual						
Lawyer A	$17,575	$14,840	118%	$ 47,000	$ 54,250	87%
Lawyer B	16,350	13,245	123%	51,325	47,990	106%
Lawyer C	12,820	14,730	87%	41,550	44,100	94%
Practice Group						
Litigation	35,110	38,990	90%	96,780	99,010	98%
Business	50,010	45,900	109%	161,070	160,200	101%
Real Estate	39,640	48,800	81%	122,221	145,960	84%
Estate Planning and Probate	24,290	23,980	101%	77,900	79,210	98%

Appendix A-4

Financial Reports

Cash and Collection Realization
March 2005

	MTD Cash	YTD Cash	Cash Rec'd in 120 days	Cash Realization
Individual				
Lawyer A	$19,360	$ 54,380	$ 41,290	88%
Lawyer B	14,100	42,190	38,430	91%
Lawyer C	9,320	31,250	24,200	77%
Practice Group				
Litigation	$32.990	$ 92,350	$ 86,345	93%
Business	47,450	150,300	149,340	99%
Real Estate	35,790	99,100	94,390	95%
Estate Planning and Probate	23,320	82,190	80,400	98%

Appendix A-5

Financial Reports

*Origination Credit
March 2005*

	MTD Billed	MTD Dollar Value	MTD Billing Realization	YTD Billed	YTD Dollar Value	YTD Billing Realization
Lawyer A	$15,255	$14,280	107%	$47,990	$44,100	109%
Lawyer B	10,230	13,240	77%	32,500	40,290	81%
Lawyer C	6,700	3,600	186%	6,700	3,600	186%

Appendix A-6

Financial Reports
Aged Work-In-Process

	Total WIP	Current WIP	30-60 Days	60-90 Days	90-360 Days	Over 360 Days
Individual						
Lawyer A	$37,340	$18,740	$ 7,250	$ 5,605	$ 2,040	$ 3,705
Lawyer B	28,900	17,590	5,770	1,450	4,090	0
Lawyer C	19,200	16,600	700	1,700	200	0
By Practice Group						
Litigation						
Hourly	$32,800	$28,900	$ 3,700	$ 200	$ 0	$ 0
Contingency	89,400	15,100	14,900	17,230	12,490	29,770
Business	52,300	46,690	4,900	0	0	710
Real Estate	42,960	35,209	7,750	0	0	1
Estate Planning and Probate	42,300	21,020	11,500	7,100	2,680	0

Appendix A-7

Financial Reports
Aged Receivables
March 2005

	Total	Current	30-60 Days	60-90 Days	90-360 Days	Over 360 Days
By Individual						
Lawyer A	$32,568	$16,230	$ 6,990	$ 760	$3,405	$5,183
Lawyer B	42,001	14,520	11,945	12,729	2,807	0
Lawyer C	18,345	12,380	5,965	0	0	0
By Practice Group						
Litigation	$45,885	$27,390	$ 9,210	$ 2,085	$7,200	$ 0
Business	49,290	38,560	9,543	1,187	0	0
Real Estate	31,110	27,540	3,566	0	4	0
Estate Planning and Probate	40,120	36,748	1,320	675	1,377	0

Appendix A-8

Financial Reports

Firm Pipeline Report
March 2005

	Value of YTD Hours Generated	WIP	Fees Billed	Billing Realization	Accounts Receivable	YTD Fees Received
Lawyer A	$45,967	$37,340	$42,356	89%	$32,568	$38,453
Lawyer B	41,290	28,900	37,890	97%	42,001	47,220
Lawyer C	35,550	19,200	36,560	83%	18,345	27,893

Appendix A-9

Financial Reports

Balance Sheet
March 2005

		<u>March 1, 2005</u>
ASSETS		
Current Assets		
Checking/Savings		
Bank of Nevada Checking	$27,341	
Bank of Nevada Savings	5,000	
IOLTA Bank of Nevada	<u>46,250</u>	
Total Checking/Savings		$ 78,591
Accounts Receivable		166,405
Other Current Assets		
Furniture	23,490	
Equipment	<u>17,930</u>	
Total Other Current Assets		41,420
Less Accumulated depreciation		(4,790)
TOTAL ASSETS		$<u>281,626</u>
LIABILITIES AND EQUITY		
Liabilities		
Current Liabilities		
Accounts Payable	$44,289	
Line of Credit	55,390	
Officer Loan	70,000	
Payroll Liabilities	6,765	
Client Funds	<u>46,250</u>	
Total Current Liabilities		$222,694
Equity		
Retained earnings		47,350
Net Income		11,582
TOTAL LIABILITIES AND EQUITY		$<u>281,626</u>

Appendix B
Financial Indicators Worksheet

Profit Ratio

$_____   divided by $_____   equals   _____%
    profit   *revenue*   *profit ratio*

Revenue per Lawyer

$_____   divided by   _____   equals $_____
    revenue   *# of lawyers*   *revenue per lawyer*

Revenue per Partner

$_____   divided by   _____   equals $_____
    revenue   *# of partners*   *revenue per partner*

Profits per Partner

$_____   divided by   _____   equals $_____
    profit   *# of partners*   *profits per partner*

Billing Realization Rate

$_____   divided by $_____   equals   _____%
    amount billed   *dollar value*   *billing*
                                   of time invested   *realization*

Billing Turnover Rate

$_____   divided by $_____   equals   _____ months
    year-end   *average billings*   *billing*
    work-in-process   *per month*   *turnover rate*

Collection Realization

$_____   divided by $_____   equals   _____%
    amount   *amount billed*   *collection*
    collected   *realization*

Collection Turnover Rate

$\underline{}$ divided by $\underline{}$ equals $\underline{}$days

   year-end   *average daily*   *collection*

   accounts   *billings*   *turnover rate*

   receivables

Volume Increase Analysis

$\underline{}$ hours times $\underline{}$ equals $\underline{}$ divided by $\underline{}$ equals $\underline{}$%

  hours   *prior year's*   *total*   *from*

  increase   *rate*   *revenue*   *additional*

                                            increase   *business*

Rate Increase Analysis

$\underline{}$ times $\underline{}$ hours equals $\underline{}$ divided by $\underline{}$ equals $\underline{}$%

increase   *total*   *total increase*   *from*

in rates   *hours*   *in revenue*   *rate*

                                                 increase

Appendix C
Revenue Capacity Worksheet

The revenue capacity of a firm is the amount of money that the firm would generate with its people working at their highest and most efficient level in the context of the firm's existing support, its present systems, its current technology, and with a sufficient amount of legal work.

A firm's revenue capacity is based on anticipated billable hours at the standard hourly rates of the lawyers and the paralegals.

Lawyers	Expected Billable Hours		Rate		Revenue
_____	_____	X	$____	=	$_____
_____	_____	X	$____	=	$_____
_____	_____	X	$____	=	$_____
_____	_____	X	$____	=	$_____
_____	_____	X	$____	=	$_____
_____	_____	X	$____	=	$_____
_____	_____	X	$____	=	$_____
_____	_____	X	$____	=	$_____
_____	_____	X	$____	=	$_____

Paralegals					
_____	_____	X	$____	=	$_____
_____	_____	X	$____	=	$_____
_____	_____	X	$____	=	$_____
_____	_____	X	$____	=	$_____
_____	_____	X	$____	=	$_____
_____	_____	X	$____	=	$_____
_____	_____	X	$____	=	$_____

Total Firm Capacity $_____

Revenue capacity is akin to "best case" and has nothing to do with actual revenue or current performance of the firm. It assumes enough work and billing and collection realization of 100 percent.

Appendix D

The Scorecard

Financial Indicator	Firm Capacity	This Year's Results	Next Year's Goal	Next Year's Results	Following Year's Goals
Revenue					
Expenses					
Partner Profit					
Profit Ratio					
Revenue per Lawyer					
Revenue per Partner					
Profit per Partner					
Hours					
Hours per Partner					
Hours per Associate					
Hours per Paralegal					
Billing Realization					
Billing Turnover					
Collection Realization					
Collection Turnover					

Appendix E

Client Intake Policies and Procedures

Part I: The Firm's Areas of Practice

The law firm recognizes that it can provide value to its clients by concentrating in the practice areas of land use and real estate litigation.

The firm accepts clients with issues in the following practice areas:

- ◆ Real Estate Litigation
- ◆ Environmental Matters
- ◆ Real Estate Development
- ◆ Zoning and Planning Board Proceedings and Appeals
- ◆ State Agency Permitting and Procedures
- ◆ Tax Abatement Applications and Appeals
- ◆ Eminent Domain Matters and Regulatory Takings

Matters not related to the above practice areas will not be accepted without the specific approval of the managing partner.

Part II: Initial Client Meeting

It is the policy of the firm to cover the following subject matters during the initial client meeting:

- ◆ Make sure there are no conflicts
- ◆ Listen to the client's story
- ◆ Relate back to the client the significant parts of the story
- ◆ Determine with specificity the client's objective
- ◆ Describe to the client the law that applies to the problem
- ◆ Share with the client the matter plan or case plan
- ◆ Identify additional needed information
- ◆ Establish the method of charging legal fees and provide client with the amount of the fee or a realistic estimate

Part III: Fee Agreements and Fee Deposits

It is the policy of the law firm to have a written fee agreement for every matter, and a fee deposit for all new clients.

- ◆ A fee agreement shall be executed with regard to every matter prior to beginning the work.
- ◆ For every new client, the lawyer shall get from the client an initial fee deposit (to be set based on the magnitude of the work to follow, but in no event less than $2,500) prior to commencing the work.
- ◆ The fee agreement will clearly designate whether the fee deposit is to be held until the end of the process or, in the alternative, utilized for payment of the ongoing periodic statements and to be replenished when exhausted.
- ◆ Exceptions to the fee deposit requirement may be made, with the approval of the managing partner, for major clients for whom it is deemed not necessary or not attainable.

Part IV: The Reality Check

The client must appreciate the difficulties and the costs of going forward.

- ◆ Have a discussion with the client at the end of the initial client meeting to be sure the client is prepared for what is to follow.
- ◆ Make a point of discussing the potential difficulties of the case and the burdens it will place on the client's life.
- ◆ Be sure the client appreciates the costs involved and is prepared to pay for your services.

Part V: Confirming the Plans

The lawyer is responsible for completing the documentation of the arrangement.

- ◆ A signed copy of the fee agreement should go to the client and a second copy to the file.
- ◆ The lawyer should acknowledge in writing the receipt of any fee deposit and the fact it is being held in the firm's trust account.
- ◆ The lawyer should send a letter covering any additional aspects of the representation that are not covered in the fee agreement. The letter should be used to further manage the client's expectations.

Appendix F

Rule 1.5: Fees

(a) A lawyer shall not make an agreement for, charge, or collect an unreasonable fee or an unreasonable amount for expenses. The factors to be considered in determining the reasonableness of a fee include the following:

   (1) the time and labor required, the novelty and difficulty of the questions involved, and the skill requisite to perform the legal service properly;

   (2) the likelihood, if apparent to the client, that the acceptance of the particular employment will preclude other employment by the lawyer;

   (3) the fee customarily charged in the locality for similar legal services;

   (4) the amount involved and the results obtained;

   (5) the time limitations imposed by the client or by the circumstances;

   (6) the nature and length of the professional relationship with the client;

   (7) the experience, reputation, and ability of the lawyer or lawyers performing the services; and

   (8) whether the fee is fixed or contingent.

(b) The scope of the representation and the basis or rate of the fee and expenses for which the client will be responsible shall be communicated to the client, preferably in writing, before or within a reasonable time after commencing the representation, except when the lawyer will charge a regularly represented client on the same basis or rate. Any changes in the basis or rate of the fee or expenses shall also be communicated to the client.

(c) A fee may be contingent on the outcome of the matter for which the service is rendered, except in a matter in which a contingent fee is prohibited by paragraph (d) or other law. A contingent fee agreement shall be in a writing signed by the client and shall state the method by which the fee

ABA Model Rule of Professional Conduct 1.5 reprinted from *Model Rules of Professional Conduct, 2004 Edition*, published by the Center for Professional Responsibility, American Bar Association, 2004. Reprinted with permission. Copies of *ABA Model Rules of Professional Conduct 2004* are available from Service Center, American Bar Association, 321 N. Clark Street, Chicago, IL 60610, 1-800-285-2221.

is to be determined, including the percentage or percentages that shall accrue to the lawyer in the event of settlement, trial or appeal; litigation and other expenses to be deducted from the recovery; and whether such expenses are to be deducted before or after the contingent fee is calculated. The agreement must clearly notify the client of any expenses for which the client will be liable whether or not the client is the prevailing party. Upon conclusion of a contingent fee matter, the lawyer shall provide the client with a written statement stating the outcome of the matter and, if there is a recovery, showing the remittance to the client and the method of its determination.

(d) A lawyer shall not enter into an arrangement for, charge, or collect:

    (1) any fee in a domestic relations matter, the payment or amount of which is contingent upon the securing of a divorce or upon the amount of alimony or support, or property settlement in lieu thereof; or

    (2) a contingent fee for representing a defendant in a criminal case.

(e) A division of a fee between lawyers who are not in the same firm may be made only if:

    (1) the division is in proportion to the services performed by each lawyer or each lawyer assumes joint responsibility for the representation;

    (2) the client agrees to the arrangement, including the share each lawyer will receive, and the agreement is confirmed in writing; and

    (3) the total fee is reasonable.

Comment

Reasonableness of Fee and Expenses

[1] Paragraph (a) requires that lawyers charge fees that are reasonable under the circumstances. The factors specified in (1) through (8) are not exclusive. Nor will each factor be relevant in each instance. Paragraph (a) also requires that expenses for which the client will be charged must be reasonable. A lawyer may seek reimbursement for the cost of services performed in-house, such as copying, or for other expenses incurred in-house, such as telephone charges, either by charging a reasonable amount to which the client has agreed in advance or by charging an amount that reasonably reflects the cost incurred by the lawyer.

Basis or Rate of Fee

[2] When the lawyer has regularly represented a client, they ordinarily will have evolved an understanding concerning the basis or rate of the fee and

the expenses for which the client will be responsible. In a new client-lawyer relationship, however, an understanding as to fees and expenses must be promptly established. Generally, it is desirable to furnish the client with at least a simple memorandum or copy of the lawyer's customary fee arrangements that states the general nature of the legal services to be provided, the basis, rate or total amount of the fee and whether and to what extent the client will be responsible for any costs, expenses or disbursements in the course of the representation. A written statement concerning the terms of the engagement reduces the possibility of misunderstanding.

[3] Contingent fees, like any other fees, are subject to the reasonableness standard of paragraph (a) of this Rule. In determining whether a particular contingent fee is reasonable, or whether it is reasonable to charge any form of contingent fee, a lawyer must consider the factors that are relevant under the circumstances. Applicable law may impose limitations on contingent fees, such as a ceiling on the percentage allowable, or may require a lawyer to offer clients an alternative basis for the fee. Applicable law also may apply to situations other than a contingent fee, for example, government regulations regarding fees in certain tax matters.

Terms of Payment

[4] A lawyer may require advance payment of a fee, but is obliged to return any unearned portion. See Rule 1.16(d). A lawyer may accept property in payment for services, such as an ownership interest in an enterprise, providing this does not involve acquisition of a proprietary interest in the cause of action or subject matter of the litigation contrary to Rule 1.8 (i). However, a fee paid in property instead of money may be subject to the requirements of Rule 1.8(a) because such fees often have the essential qualities of a business transaction with the client.

[5] An agreement may not be made whose terms might induce the lawyer improperly to curtail services for the client or perform them in a way contrary to the client's interest. For example, a lawyer should not enter into an agreement whereby services are to be provided only up to a stated amount when it is foreseeable that more extensive services probably will be required, unless the situation is adequately explained to the client. Otherwise, the client might have to bargain for further assistance in the midst of a proceeding or transaction. However, it is proper to define the extent of services in light of the client's ability to pay. A lawyer should not exploit a fee arrangement based primarily on hourly charges by using wasteful procedures.

Prohibited Contingent Fees

[6] Paragraph (d) prohibits a lawyer from charging a contingent fee in a domestic relations matter when payment is contingent upon the securing of a

divorce or upon the amount of alimony or support or property settlement to be obtained. This provision does not preclude a contract for a contingent fee for legal representation in connection with the recovery of postjudgment balances due under support, alimony or other financial orders because such contracts do not implicate the same policy concerns.

Division of Fee

[7] A division of fee is a single billing to a client covering the fee of two or more lawyers who are not in the same firm. A division of fee facilitates association of more than one lawyer in a matter in which neither alone could serve the client as well, and most often is used when the fee is contingent and the division is between a referring lawyer and a trial specialist. Paragraph (e) permits the lawyers to divide a fee either on the basis of the proportion of services they render or if each lawyer assumes responsibility for the representation as a whole. In addition, the client must agree to the arrangement, including the share that each lawyer is to receive, and the agreement must be confirmed in writing. Contingent fee agreements must be in a writing signed by the client and must otherwise comply with paragraph (c) of this Rule. Joint responsibility for the representation entails financial and ethical responsibility for the representation as if the lawyers were associated in a partnership. A lawyer should only refer a matter to a lawyer whom the referring lawyer reasonably believes is competent to handle the matter. See Rule 1.1.

[8] Paragraph (e) does not prohibit or regulate division of fees to be received in the future for work done when lawyers were previously associated in a law firm.

Disputes over Fees

[9] If a procedure has been established for resolution of fee disputes, such as an arbitration or mediation procedure established by the bar, the lawyer must comply with the procedure when it is mandatory, and, even when it is voluntary, the lawyer should conscientiously consider submitting to it. Law may prescribe a procedure for determining a lawyer's fee, for example, in representation of an executor or administrator, a class or a person entitled to a reasonable fee as part of the measure of damages. The lawyer entitled to such a fee and a lawyer representing another party concerned with the fee should comply with the prescribed procedure.

Appendix G-1

Law Firm Plan for Implementing Value-Based Billing

Document Preparation

Identify Document _____

FIRST, take a look at the investment of the law firm in preparing the document:

- ◆ Estimate the investment of lawyer and paralegal time involved in client meetings, gathering information, and communications based on standard hourly rates.　　　　$_____

- ◆ Determine the investment of lawyer and paralegal time in the preparation of the document, taking advantage of previously created forms and document assembly programs.　　　　$_____

- ◆ Consider the value to the client of the intellectual property that went into the creation of the forms utilized.　　　　$_____

- ◆ Consider the incremental value that the investment in technology brings to the project.　　　　$_____

Add the above components to determine the total value based on the law firm's investment.　　　　$_____

NEXT, take a look at the value to the client:

- ◆ Put yourself in the shoes of your client and try to come up with the value of the work product to the client. (This is subjective and not easy, so think about it in terms of a range.)　　from $_____ to $_____
　　　　　　　　　　　　　　　　　　low　　　　*high*

◆ Based on your sense of the competition
   in the marketplace, what is the range of
   fees charged for similar services?   from $_____ to $_____

                                                     low   *high*

THEN, do a reconciliation of the numbers developed and add an
overlay of judgment to establish the fixed price for the service:

   Value based solely on law firm investment $_____
   Value of work product from the client's perspective $_____ to $_____
   Range of fees charged by others $_____ to $_____

The overlay of judgment means you are using the numbers as background information, but in the last analysis the question of what is a fair fee for the service your firm provides to your clients is subjective.

Appendix G-2

Law Firm Plan for Implementing Value-Based Billing

The Fixed Fee for Small Case

Identify Type of Case _____

FIRST, create a case plan, breaking the matter down into component parts and, based on standard hourly rates, project the hourly fee for each such component, using a range of dollars to recognize the differences in cases.

Investigation	Lawyer		Paralegal		
_____	$_____		$_____		
_____	$_____		$_____		
_____	$_____		$_____		
_____	$_____		$_____		
Total for this phase	$_____	+	$_____	=	$_____

Initiate or Respond to Litigation	Lawyer		Paralegal		
_____	$_____		$_____		
_____	$_____		$_____		
_____	$_____		$_____		
_____	$_____		$_____		
Total for this phase	$_____	+	$_____	=	$_____

Discovery	Lawyer		Paralegal		
_____	$_____		$_____		
_____	$_____		$_____		
_____	$_____		$_____		
_____	$_____		$_____		
Total for this phase	$_____	+	$_____	=	$_____

Motions, Hearings, Other

_____	$_____	$_____
_____	$_____	$_____
_____	$_____	$_____
_____	$_____	$_____

Total for this phase $_____   + $_____   = $_____

Final Trial Preparation

_____	$_____	$_____
_____	$_____	$_____
_____	$_____	$_____

Total for this phase $_____   + $_____   = $_____

Trial $_____   + $_____   = $_____

TOTAL based on best estimates of work at standard
hourly rates $_____

NEXT, review five to eight completed files and compare the actual investment of time (or total hourly fee) in similar matters.

completed matter	_fee_
_____	$_____
_____	$_____
_____	$_____
_____	$_____
_____	$_____
_____	$_____
_____	$_____
_____	$_____

Range of fees in similar matters   from $_____ to $_____
         low   _high_

THEN, evaluate how the completed matters could
have been produced more efficiently and more
productively and adjust estimates of proposed
fee as appropriate.   from $_____ to $_____
         low   _high_

THEN, put yourself in the shoes of the client and
try to come up with a value of the work product
to the client.   from $_____ to $_____
         low   _high_

THEN, do a reconciliation of the guidance numbers:

Estimate based on standard hourly rates $_____

Estimate range based on review of completed
files   from $_____ to $_____
                                                                   low   *high*

Estimate of value from client's perspective   from $_____ to $_____
                                                                   low   *high*

FINALLY, give consideration to the guidance numbers
and add an overlay of judgment to come up with a
fixed fee for the services to be performed. $_____

Note: As in any matter handled for a fixed fee, the description of the services to be performed for the fee is critical. This is particularly important in litigated matters where it is necessary to address the circumstances under which an unexpected turn of events would cause the fee arrangement to be revisited.

Appendix G-3

Law Firm Plan for Implementing Value-Based Billing

Transactional Matter

Identify Type of Matter _____

FIRST, create a plan, breaking down the matter into component parts and, based on standard hourly rates, project the hourly fee for each such components.

	Lawyer		Paralegal		
Initial Client Meeting and Developing Strategy					
_____	$_____		$_____		
_____	$_____		$_____		
Total for this phase	$_____	+	$_____	=	$_____
Collection of Information					
_____	$_____		$_____		
_____	$_____		$_____		
_____	$_____		$_____		
_____	$_____		$_____		
Total for this phase	$_____	+	$_____	=	$_____
Drafting of Documents					
_____	$_____		$_____		
_____	$_____		$_____		
_____	$_____		$_____		
Total for this phase	$_____	+	$_____	=	$_____
Developing Closing Statement	$_____	+	$_____	=	$_____

Closing $\$\underline{\hspace{1cm}}$ + $\$\underline{\hspace{1cm}}$ = $\$\underline{\hspace{1.5cm}}$

Post Closing Work $\$\underline{\hspace{1cm}}$ + $\$\underline{\hspace{1cm}}$ = $\$\underline{\hspace{1.5cm}}$

Total based on best estimates of work at standard
hourly rates $\$\underline{\hspace{1cm}}$

NEXT, review 5 to 8 completed files and compare the actual investment of time (or total hourly fee) in similar matters.

completed matter	*fee*
_____	$\$\underline{\hspace{1cm}}$
_____	$\$\underline{\hspace{1cm}}$
_____	$\$\underline{\hspace{1cm}}$
_____	$\$\underline{\hspace{1cm}}$
_____	$\$\underline{\hspace{1cm}}$
_____	$\$\underline{\hspace{1cm}}$
_____	$\$\underline{\hspace{1cm}}$
_____	$\$\underline{\hspace{1cm}}$

Range of fees in similar matters   from $\$\underline{\hspace{1cm}}$ to $\$\underline{\hspace{1cm}}$
                                                      low   *high*

THEN, evaluate how the completed matters could
have been produced more efficiently and more
productively and adjust estimates of proposed
fee as appropriate.   from $\$\underline{\hspace{1cm}}$ to $\$\underline{\hspace{1cm}}$
                                                      low   *high*

THEN, put yourself in the shoes of the client and
try to come up with a value of the work product
to the client.   from $\$\underline{\hspace{1cm}}$ to $\$\underline{\hspace{1cm}}$
                                                      low   *high*

THEN, do a reconciliation of the guidance numbers:

Estimate based on standard hourly rates $\$\underline{\hspace{1cm}}$
Estimate range based on review of completed
files   from $\$\underline{\hspace{1cm}}$ to $\$\underline{\hspace{1cm}}$
                                                      low   *high*
Estimate of value from client's perspective   from $\$\underline{\hspace{1cm}}$ to $\$\underline{\hspace{1cm}}$
                                                      low   *high*

FINALLY, give consideration to the guidance numbers
and add an overlay of judgment to come up with a
fixed fee for the services to be performed. $\$\underline{\hspace{1cm}}$

Appendix H
Sample Billable Hour Policy

Basic Policy

In order to assist firm in revenue budgeting, the firm has adopted annual billable hour goals [requirements] [commitments] for its Directors, Associates, and Paralegals:

Partners	1,600 Billable Hours
Associates	1,750 Billable Hours
Paralegals	1,450 Billable Hours

Meeting or exceeding the billable hour goals [requirements][commitments] will be one factor considered by the firm in its annual evaluation and compensation process.

Optional Provisions:

- Any individual variations from these goals [requirements] [commitments] for people with part-time schedules or other circumstances shall be allowed if approved by the Practice Group Leader and the firm's Administrator.
- Partners, Associates, and Paralegals with a part-time schedule shall have their billable hour goals [requirements][commitments] reduced on a *pro rata* basis.
- The Managing Partner's goals [requirements][commitments] shall be reduced by 50%.
- The firm is committed to *pro bono* work and up to _____ hours of *pro bono* hours a year can be counted toward the individual's billable hour goal [requirement] [commitment].
- The firm is committed to *pro bono* work and expects each of its lawyers to accept and handle *pro bono* cases, which are considered an obligation over and above their individual billable hour goal [requirement] [commitment] set by the firm.

Appendix I

Sample Time Recording Policy

It is critical to the successful operation of the law firm that billable time be recorded daily and submitted to the time and billing system. Delays in recording time inevitably result in the loss of revenue and delays in submitting time to the system frequently cause time to be written off if it arrives in the system after the client has been billed. Delays are particularly problematic when more than one timekeeper is working on a file. The loss of revenue can be substantial.

In order to avoid loss of revenue, it is the policy of this firm that all time be recorded on the same day the work is performed and that the time be submitted to the system no later than 10am on the day following the performance of the work.

Please have in mind that the words you use on your time entries often appear on the client's bill and must justify the charges made. The bill becomes a communication tool and the time entries need to convey a sense of value, or information describing what has been accomplished. Brief descriptions of mechanical functions (such as research law, office conference, telephone call) without more detail must be avoided.

Appendix J

Variable Hourly Rate Worksheet

Lawyer _____

    Standard Hourly Rate $_____

    Special Rate Work
        (Premium and Discount)

        _____ $_____

        _____ $_____

        _____ $_____

        _____ $_____

        _____ $_____

    History

        Average hourly rate

            1999 $_____

            2000 $_____

            2001 $_____

            2002 $_____

            2003 $_____

            2004 $_____

Appendix K

Sample Client-Centered Service Policy

The Firm's Client-Centered Service Policy is based on a recognition that what clients want most from their lawyers is care and concern. Often, satisfaction is based more on how the client is treated than the result obtained or the amount of the fee.

Part I: General Principles

Lawyers and staff shall endeavor to give priority to the following principles in their client relationships:

- ◆ Representation of a client is an interactive process
- ◆ The lawyer and the entire staff must develop and consistently maintain a mindset that *it is all about the client*
- ◆ Clients should be treated as people, not files
- ◆ Responding to client contacts should be given priority
- ◆ Every client contact by all staff should project genuine concern for the client's issue

Part II: Telephone Communications

Communications with the client should be regular and consistent with the expectations established with the client during intake. Responses to client initiated contacts should be prompt and meaningful.

- ◆ Client communication should meet the client's need and expectation
- ◆ Clients should receive information about significant events or changes promptly
- ◆ Communicating bad news should be a priority and should never be delayed
- ◆ Client telephone calls should be returned within two hours, and if that is impossible, a staff member should return the call to explain the delay and find a way to get help if there is a need for immediate attention

- Lawyers should return all calls on the same day, even if it means a return call during evening hours

Part III: Correspondence

Written communication with the client may include traditional correspondence, faxes, or e-mail messages.

- Clients should receive copies of documents and pleadings, with a letter should the enclosure need explanation
- Clients should receive status reports monthly, unless some other arrangement has been made
- E-mail may be used for brief messages, but should not be used for confidential information or a significant communication

Part IV: Communications Through the Billing Process

The billing process is an excellent client communication tool.

- Time entries on itemized bills should avoid reciting mechanical functions and rather should be used to communicate substantive accomplishments and value provided
- Monthly bills should be sent with a cover letter briefly summarizing the work performed and the work planned for the following month

Part V: Managing Client Expectations

The client's expectations must be managed throughout the process.

- Any significant change in the course of a matter or a case plan must be shared with the client at the earliest possible time
- The case plan and any fee estimate should be easily accessible and referred to regularly during the course of a matter
- Lawyers and staff need to be familiar with the case plan and fee estimate as everyone needs to cooperate in managing a case within the parameters of the client's expectations
- At the time of monthly billing, the lawyer should refer to the fee estimate
- If the fee estimate cannot be met, the lawyer needs to adjust the matter in which the matter is handled or contact the client to discuss adjusting the amount of the estimate

◆ Contact a client in advance if a monthly bill is higher than the client expects, thereby being careful never to surprise a client with the amount of a bill

Part VI: Recovery

If a client has a problem or becomes unhappy with some aspect of the service, the situation should be addressed as soon as possible so that the matter will not fester.

◆ If a client calls and leaves a message expressing unhappiness with some aspect of the service, the return of the phone call must have the highest priority

◆ Staff members who are aware of a telephone message in which a client expresses unhappiness with some aspect of the service must get word of the call to the lawyer ASAP (and not simply leave the message on the lawyer's desk)

◆ Never delay returning a call to a client who has left a message expressing unhappiness with any aspect of the service

Appendix L
Sample Paralegal Hiring Policy

To be considered for a paralegal position in the firm, the applicant must have the following minimum qualifications:

1. The applicant must have oral and written communication skills, interpersonal skills, technology and research skills, and organizational skills.
2. The applicant must take pride in his or her work and be thorough and detail-oriented.
3. The applicant must be a good match for the personalities of the lawyers and be someone with whom the clients would have confidence.
4. The applicant should have no less than three (3) years paralegal experience in a law firm or similar organization.
5. The applicant's educational background should include a degree from a four- [two-] year college with either a major in paralegal studies or a related subject, or a post-graduation certificate in paralegal studies.
   [Optional provision providing for an exception: the firm may waive the educational requirement for existing employees with ten or more years with the firm who have exhibited an exceptional knowledge and value in one of the firm's practice areas.]
   [A different education provision: the applicant must have graduated from an ABA-approved paralegal program.]
6. The Certified Legal Assistant (CLA) offered by the National Association of Legal Assistants is required [considered desirable].

Note: the policy sets out minimum skills for paralegals. The skills needed for a particular position should be set out in more detail as they will depend on the specific demands of the practice area. A litigation paralegal may need a different skill set than a probate or estate planning paralegal.

Appendix M

Paralegal Profitability Worksheet

Quick Check

A quick check on whether a paralegal is profitable can be conducted using the *rule of three*.[1] Under this analysis, the revenue attributed to the paralegal should be three times his or her salary. For each paralegal, conduct the following analysis:

Calculate the revenue attributed to the paralegal:

_____ hours times $____ equals $_____ less $_____ equals $_____
hours   *rate*   *capacity*   *write-offs*   *revenue*
                                                          converted to $

Compare the one-third of revenue to the paralegal's salary:

One-third revenue $_____
Salary $_____

Specific Analysis

Given more time, a careful analysis can be conducted in which the actual costs of maintaining the paralegal can be performed. To conduct this analysis, determine as best you can the actual cost of the paralegal:

Salary $_____
Fringe benefits $_____
Share of secretarial support $_____
Share of space $_____

---

[1]The *rule of three* continues to be a good guide in small and midsized firms with a reasonable overhead cost. For firms with high overhead it is better to run a specific cost analysis to determine whether the firm should be looking for greater profits from their paralegals.

Furniture and equipment amortized $_____

_____ $_____

_____ $_____

Other costs $_____

     Total costs $_____

Then run the *rule of three* utilizing actual costs

$_____ **less** $_____ **equals** $_____

  revenue attributed   *cost of maintaining*   *profit*

    to paralegal   *paralegal*

Appendix N
Paralegal Billing Guidelines

These guidelines are to assist paralegals and legal assistants in knowing what functions are properly billable to the client and which functions are more appropriately part of the lawyer's hourly rate.

The best description of what functions are billable was publicized in the 1980s when the ABA welcomed legal assistants as associate members. In the process, the ABA adopted the following definition of legal assistants:

> . . . persons, qualified through education, training, or work experience, who are employed . . . by a lawyer . . . which involves the performance, under the ultimate direction and supervision of an attorney, of specifically delegated substantive legal work, which work, for the most part, requires sufficient knowledge of legal concepts that, absent such assistant, the attorney would perform the task. (emphasis added)

The courts have latched onto the ABA definition in fee-shifting cases and there have been many decisions that discuss the difference between delegated substantive legal work and clerical work (which is properly considered part of the firm's overhead).

The following functions are examples of work considered billable if performed by a legal assistant under the supervision of a lawyer:

- Participate in client meetings
- Manage the exchange of information with client
- Assist clients in completing forms
- Draft fact memos
- Draft status letters to client
- Draft letters to opposing counsel or others
- Perform document assembly functions
- Assist clients with the execution of documents
- Draft deeds and other real estate documents
- Prepare closing agendas
- Handle closings
- Prepare corporate documents
- Assist with corporate filings

- ◆ Maintain corporate records
- ◆ Conduct investigations
- ◆ Collect records
- ◆ Conduct witness interviews
- ◆ Prepare summaries
- ◆ Review and analyze medical records
- ◆ Manage complex files
- ◆ Prepare drafts of pleadings
- ◆ Prepare drafts of discovery documents
- ◆ Conduct expert searches
- ◆ Work with experts to provide material for review
- ◆ Assist in preparing deposition outlines
- ◆ Assist lawyer in deposition
- ◆ Conduct factual and medical research
- ◆ Conduct legal research
- ◆ Create trial notebooks
- ◆ Assist in trial preparation
- ◆ Provide support at trial

The firm does not charge clients for receiving letters and documents, reviewing letters and documents to determine where to file them, filing, typing basic cover letters, typing letters dictated by others, making appointments, scheduling, and photocopying. These are examples of functions that should not be recorded as billable time.

Any questions about what should recorded as billable should be directed to the appropriate practice group leader or the paralegal manager.

Appendix O

Sample Law Firm Collection Policy

The law firm has adopted these policies to provide a consistent and effective collection policy.

1. There shall be a signed fee agreement in every file prior to commencing work on the matter. The fee agreement shall specifically provide that timely payment for legal services is required.
2. At the time of intake, the lawyer shall let the client know that if the client ever has a problem paying a bill within thirty days, the client should call the lawyer to discuss the matter. This requirement should be reinforced in the fee agreement or in the cover letter enclosing the fee agreement.
3. Any bill going to a client with a back due balance shall include a letter stating that the past due balance is unacceptable and must be paid immediately.
4. Should the back-due balance not be paid by day 45, either the lawyer or a designated staff member should call the client to request payment.
5. If agreement cannot be reached, or agreement is reached but payment is not received, then there should be a second call to the client setting up a meeting with the lawyer to reevaluate the relationship.
6. At the meeting, the lawyer and client should consider restructuring the fee agreement, make a change in the plan or objective based on cost considerations, or (if ethically permissible) terminating the representation.

Appendix P

Planning Worksheet

To Do	Date	Responsible Person

1. Work with Financial Indicators
- Develop maximum capacity and insert in scorecard _____ _____
- Develop financial indicators for prior year _____ _____
- Fill in prior year's results on scorecard _____ _____
- Set goals for next year's goals and insert on scorecard _____ _____

2. Paralegals
- Adopt paralegal hiring policy _____ _____
- Complete paralegal profitability worksheet _____ _____

3. Billable Hours Matters
- Adopt time recording policy _____ _____
- Complete variable hourly rate form for each lawyer _____ _____
- Adopt billable hour policy _____ _____

4. Client Intake Policies and Procedures
- Develop first draft by _____ _____
- Discussion at meeting on _____ _____
- Revisions to be completed by _____ _____
- To be adopted at meeting on _____ _____

5. Client-Centered Service Policy
- Develop first draft by _____ _____
- Discussion at meeting on _____ _____
- Revisions to be completed by _____ _____
- To be adopted by _____ _____

6. Billing Methods
   - Initiate pilot programs for alternative billing methods in each practice group _____ _____
   - Each practice group completes pilot program planning _____ _____
   - Each practice group adopts alternative fee agreements _____ _____
   - Review results of pilot programs _____ _____
   - Expand pilot programs _____ _____

7. Law Firm Collection Policy
   - Develop first draft by _____ _____
   - Discussion at meeting on _____ _____
   - Revisions to be completed by _____ _____
   - To be adopted by _____ _____

8. Evaluate Progress on Improving Revenue _____ _____

Resources

Calloway, James A., and Robertson, Mark A. *Winning Alternatives to the Billable Hour: Strategies That Work, Second Edition.* Chicago: American Bar Association, 2002.

Durham, James A., and McMurray, Deborah, editors. *The Lawyer's Guide to Marketing Your Practice, Second Edition.* Chicago: American Bar Association, 2004.

Ewalt, Henry W. *Through the Client's Eyes: New Approaches to Get Clients to Hire You Again and Again, Second Edition.* Chicago: American Bar Association, 2002.

Foonberg, Jay G. *The ABA Guide to Lawyer Trust Accounts.* Chicago: American Bar Association, 1996.

Greene, Arthur G. *Leveraging with Legal Assistants: How to Maximize Team Performance, Improve Quality, and Boost Your Bottom Line.* Chicago: American Bar Association, 1993.

Greene, Arthur G., and Cannon, Therese A. *Paralegals, Profitability, and the Future of Your Law Practice.* Chicago: American Bar Association, 2003.

Grella, Thomas C., and Hudkins, Michael L. *The Lawyer's Guide to Strategic Planning: Defining, Setting, and Achieving Your Firm's Goals.* Chicago: American Bar Association, 2004.

Morgan, J. Harris, and Foonberg, Jay G. *How to Draft Bills Clients Rush to Pay, Second Edition,* Chicago: American Bar Association, 2003.

Munneke, Gary A., and Davis, Anthony E. *The Essential Formbook: Comprehensive Management Tools for Lawyers, Volume I: Partnership and Organizational Agreements/Client*

Intake and Fee Agreements. Chicago: American Bar Association, 2000, 2003.

Munneke, Gary A., and Davis, Anthony E. *The Essential Formbook: Comprehensive Management Tools for Lawyers, Volume II: Human Resources/ Fees, Billing, and Collection*. Chicago: American Bar Association, 2001.

Munneke, Gary A., and Davis, Anthony E. *The Essential Formbook: Comprehensive Management Tools for Lawyers, Volume III: Calendar, Docket, and File Management/Law Firm Financial Analysis*. Chicago: American Bar Association, 2003.

Munneke, Gary A., and Davis, Anthony E. *The Essential Formbook: Comprehensive Management Tools for Lawyers, Volume IV: Disaster Planning and Recovery/Risk Management and Professional Liability Insurance*. Chicago: American Bar Association, 2004.

Poll, Edward. *Collecting Your Fee: Getting Paid From Intake to Invoice*. Chicago: American Bar Association, 2002.

Randall, Kerry. *Effective Yellow Pages Advertising for Lawyers: The Complete Guide to Creating Winning Ads*. Chicago: American Bar Association, 2002.

Shannon, Marcia Pennington, and Manch, Susan G. *Recruiting Lawyers: How to Hire the Best Talent*. Chicago: American Bar Association, 2000.

Vogt, M. Diane, and Rickard, Lori-Ann. *Keeping Good Lawyers: Best Practices to Create Career Satisfaction*. Chicago: American Bar Association, 2000.

Index

The Essential Formbook:
Comprehensive Management Tools for Lawyers
Volume I: Partnership and Organizational
Agreements/Client Intake and Fee Agreements
Volume II: Human Resources/
Fees, Billing, and Collection
Volume III: Calendar and File Management/
Law Firm Financial Analysis
Volume IV: Disaster Planning and Recovery/
Risk Management and Professional Liability Insurance
By Gary A. Munneke and Anthony E. Davis
Useful to legal practitioners of all specialties and sizes,
these volumes will help you establish profitable, affir-
mative client relationships so you can avoid unneces-
sary risks associated with malpractice and disciplinary
complaints. And, with all the forms available on CD-
ROM, it's easy to modify them to match your specific
needs. Visit our Web site at www.lawpractice.org/cata-
log/511-0424 for more information about this invaluable resource.

The Lawyer's Guide to Strategic Planning:
Defining, Setting, and Achieving Your Firm's Goals
By Thomas C. Grella and Michael L. Hudkins
This practice-building resource is your guide to planning dynamic strategic plans and implementing them
at your firm. You'll learn about the actual planning
process and how to establish goals in key planning
areas such as law firm governance, competition, opening a new office, financial management, technology,
marketing and competitive intelligence, client development and retention, and more. The accompanying CD-
ROM contains a wealth of policies, statements, and
other sample documents. If you're serious about
improving the way your firm works, increasing productivity, making better decisions, and setting your firm
on the right course—this is the resource you need.

Anatomy of a Law Firm Merger:
How to Make or Break the Deal,
Third Edition
By Hildebrandt International
How can you effectively navigate the merger process?
This updated Third Edition can help you decide when
to consider a merger and how to make the many other
decisions involved in completing the merger and ultimately integrating the merged firm. This resource will
help you to consider the right and wrong reasons to
merge, analyze strengths and weaknesses, and formu-
late specific goals for the merger. The book also contains valuable exhibits, questionnaires, and checklists—furnished in text and CD-ROM formats.

Unbundling Legal Services:
A Guide to Delivering Legal Services a la Carte
By Forrest S. Mosten
Unbundling, the practice of supplying the client dis-
crete lawyering tasks according to the client's direction, is changing the face of the legal profession today.
Given minor modifications, any firm can start
unbundling their law practice and offer this new con-
sumer-oriented approach to legal service delivery to
their clients. Learn how to set up and manage an
unbundling law practice, get new clients, and market
this new area of your practice. Offered as a supple-
ment to a traditional full-service practice, you will
recapture market share and gain professional satisfaction by offering this innovative service.

The ABA Guide to Lawyer Trust Accounts
By Jay G Foonberg
Avoid the pitfalls of trust account rules violations!
Designed as a self-study course or as seminar materials, with short, stand-alone chapters that walk you
through the procedures of client trust accounting. This
indispensable reference outlines the history of applicable ethics rules; how you could inadvertently be violat-
ing those rules; ways to work with your banker and
accountant to set up the office systems you need;
numerous forms that you can adapt for your office
(including self-tests for seminars and CLE credits); plus
Foonberg's "10 rules of good trust account procedures"
and "10 steps to good trust account records"—intended to work with whatever local rules your state man-
dates.

The Lawyer's Guide to Marketing Your Practice,
Second Edition
Edited by James A. Durham and Deborah McMurray
This book is packed with practical ideas, innovative
strategies, useful checklists, and sample marketing and
action plans to help you implement a successful, multi-
faceted, and profit-enhancing marketing plan for your
firm. Organized into four sections, this illuminating
resource covers: Developing Your Approach;
Enhancing Your Image; Implementing Marketing
Strategies and Maintaining Your Program. Appendix
materials include an instructive primer on market
research to inform you on research methodologies that
support the marketing of legal services. The accompanying CD-ROM contains a wealth of checklists, plans,
and other sample reports, questionnaires, and tem-
plates—all designed to make implementing your marketing strategy as easy as
possible.

30-Day Risk-Free Order Form
Call Today! 1-800-285-2221
Monday–Friday, 7:30 AM – 5:30 PM, Central Time

Qty	Title	LPM Price	Regular Price	Total
_____	ABA Guide to Lawyer Trust Accounts (5110374)	$ 69.95	$ 79.95	$_____
_____	Anatomy of a Law Firm Merger, Third Edition (5110506)	79.95	94.95	$_____
_____	Collecting Your Fee: Getting Paid From Intake to Invoice (5110490)	69.95	79.95	$_____
_____	The Essential Formbook, Volume I (5110424V1)	169.95	199.95	$_____
_____	The Essential Formbook, Volume II (5110424V2)	169.95	199.95	$_____
_____	The Essential Formbook, Volume III (5110424V3)	169.95	199.95	$_____
_____	The Essential Formbook, Volume IV (5110424V4)	169.95	199.95	$_____
_____	How to Draft Bills Clients Rush to Pay, Second Edition (5110495)	57.95	67.95	$_____
_____	The Lawyer's Guide to Adobe Acrobat (5110512)	49.95	59.95	$_____
_____	The Lawyer's Guide to Marketing Your Practice, Second Edition (5110500)	79.95	89.95	$_____
_____	The Lawyer's Guide to Strategic Planning (5110520)	59.95	79.95	$_____
_____	Paralegals, Profitability, and the Future of Your Law Practice (5110491)	59.95	69.95	$_____
_____	Results-Oriented Financial Management, Second Edition (5110493)	89.95	99.95	$_____
_____	Unbundling Legal Services (5110448)	54.95	64.95	$_____
_____	Winning Alternatives to the Billable Hour, Second Edition (5110483)	129.95	149.95	$_____

*Postage and Handling	
$10.00 to $24.99	$5.95
$25.00 to $49.99	$9.95
$50.00 to $99.99	$12.95
$100.00 to $349.99	$17.95
$350 to $499.99	$24.95

**Tax
DC residents add 5.75%
IL residents add 8.75%
MD residents add 5%

*Postage and Handling	$_____
**Tax	$_____
TOTAL	$_____

PAYMENT

❑ Check enclosed (to the ABA)

❑ Visa   ❑ MasterCard   ❑ American Express

_____
Account Number   Exp. Date   Signature

Name _____ Firm _____

Address _____

City _____ State _____ Zip _____

Phone Number _____ E-Mail Address _____

Note: E-Mail address is required if ordering the
The Lawyer's Guide to Fact Finding on the Internet
E-mail Newsletter (5110498)

Guarantee

If—for any reason—you are not satisfied with your purchase, you may return it within 30 days of receipt for a complete refund of the price of the book(s). No questions asked!

Mail: ABA Publication Orders, P.O. Box 10892, Chicago, Illinois 60610-0892
♦ Phone: 1-800-285-2221 ♦ FAX: 312-988-5568

E-Mail: abasvcctr@abanet.org ♦ Internet: http://www.lawpractice.org/catalog

LawPracticeManagementSection
MARKETING • MANAGEMENT • TECHNOLOGY • FINANCE

JOIN the ABA Law Practice Management Section (LPM) and receive significant discounts on future LPM book purchases! You'll also get direct access to marketing, management, technology, and finance tools that help lawyers and other professionals meet the demands of today's challenging legal environment.

Exclusive Membership Benefits Include:

- **Law Practice Magazine**
  Eight annual issues of our award-winning *Law Practice* magazine, full of insightful articles and practical tips on Marketing/Client Development, Practice Management, Legal Technology, and Finance.
- **ABA TECHSHOW®**
  Receive a $100 discount on ABA TECHSHOW, the world's largest legal technology conference!
- **LPM Book Discount**
  LPM has over eighty titles in print! Books topics cover the four core areas of law practice management – marketing, management, technology, and finance – as well as legal career issues.
- **Law Practice Today**
  LPM's unique web-based magazine in which the features change weekly! Law Practice Today covers all the hot topics in law practice management *today* – current issues, current challenges, current solutions.
- **Discounted CLE & Other Educational Opportunities**
  The Law Practice Management Section sponsors more than 100 educational sessions annually. LPM also offers other live programs, teleconferences and web cast seminars.
- **LawPractice.news**
  This monthly eUpdate brings information on Section news and activities, educational opportunities, and details on book releases and special offers.

Complete the membership application below.

Applicable Dues:
o$40 for ABA members   o$5 for ABA Law Student Division members

  (ABA Membership is a prerequisite to membership in the Section. To join the ABA, call the Service Center at 1-800-285-2221.)

Method of Payment:
oBill me   Charge to my: oVisa   oMasterCard   oAmerican Express
Card number _____ Exp. Date _____
Signature _____ Date _____

Applicant's Information (please print):
Name _____ ABA I.D. number _____
Firm/Organization _____
Address _____ City/State/Zip _____
Telephone _____FAX_____ Email _____

Fax your application to 312-988-5528 or join by phone: 1-800-285-2221, TDD 312-988-5168
Join online at www.lawpractice.org.

I understand that my membership dues include $16 for a basic subscription to *Law Practice Management* magazine. This subscription charge is not deductible from the dues and additional subscriptions are not available at this rate. Membership dues in the American Bar Association and its Sections are not deductible as charitable contributions for income tax purposes but may be deductible as a business expense.

About the CD

The accompanying CD contains the text of each of the Appendices (excluding Appendix F) from *The Lawyer's Guide to Increasing Revenue.* The files are in Microsoft Word® and Excel® formats.

For additional information about the files on the CD, please open and read the "**readme.doc**" file on the CD.

NOTE: The set of files on the CD may only be used on a single computer or moved to and used on another computer. Under no circumstances may the set of files be used on more than one computer at one time. If you are interested in obtaining a license to use the set of files on a local network, please contact: Director, Copyrights and Contracts, American Bar Association, 321 N. Clark Street, Chicago, IL 60610, (312) 988-6101. **Please read the license and warranty statements on the following page before using this CD.**

CD-ROM to accompany
The Lawyer's Guide to Increasing Revenue

WARNING: Opening this package indicates your understanding and acceptance of the following Terms and Conditions.

READ THE FOLLOWING TERMS AND CONDITIONS BEFORE OPENING THIS SEALED PACKAGE. IF YOU DO NOT AGREE WITH THEM, PROMPTLY RETURN THE UNOPENED PACKAGE TO EITHER THE PARTY FROM WHOM IT WAS ACQUIRED OR TO THE AMERICAN BAR ASSOCIATION AND YOUR MONEY WILL BE RETURNED.

The document files in this package are a proprietary product of the American Bar Association and are protected by Copyright Law. The American Bar Association retains title to and ownership of these files.

License

You may use this set of files on a single computer or move it to and use it on another computer, but under no circumstances may you use the set of files on more than one computer at the same time. You may copy the files either in support of your use of the files on a single computer or for backup purposes. If you are interested in obtaining a license to use the set of files on a local network, please contact: Manager, Publication Policies & Contracting, American Bar Association, 312 N. Clark Street, Chicago, IL 60610, (312) 988-6101.

You may permanently transfer the set of files to another party if the other party agrees to accept the terms and conditions of this License Agreement. If you transfer the set of files, you must at the same time transfer all copies of the files to the same party or destroy those not transferred. Such transfer terminates your license. You may not rent, lease, assign or otherwise transfer the files except as stated in this paragraph.

You may modify these files for your own use within the provisions of this License Agreement. You may not redistribute any modified files.

Warranty

If a CD-ROM in this package is defective, the American Bar Association will replace it at no charge if the defective diskette is returned to the American Bar Association within 60 days from the date of acquisition.

American Bar Association warrants that these files will perform in substantial compliance with the documentation supplied in this package. However, the American Bar Association does not warrant these forms as to the correctness of the legal material contained therein. If you report a significant defect in performance in writing to the American Bar Association, and the American Bar Association is not able to correct it within 60 days, you may return the CD, including all copies and documentation, to the American Bar Association and the American Bar Association will refund your money.

Any files that you modify will no longer be covered under this warranty even if they were modified in accordance with the License Agreement and product documentation.

IN NO EVENT WILL THE AMERICAN BAR ASSOCIATION, ITS OFFICERS, MEMBERS, OR EMPLOYEES BE LIABLE TO YOU FOR ANY DAMAGES, INCLUDING LOST PROFITS, LOST SAVINGS OR OTHER INCIDENTAL OR CONSEQUENTIAL DAMAGES ARISING OUT OF YOUR USE OR INABILITY TO USE THESE FILES EVEN IF THE AMERICAN BAR ASSOCIATION OR AN AUTHORIZED AMERICAN BAR ASSOCIATION REPRESENTATIVE HAS BEEN ADVISED OF THE POSSIBILITY OF SUCH DAMAGES, OR FOR ANY CLAIM BY ANY OTHER PARTY. SOME STATES DO NOT ALLOW THE LIMITATION OR EXCLUSION OF LIABILITY FOR INCIDENTAL OR CONSEQUENTIAL DAMAGES, IN WHICH CASE THIS LIMITATION MAY NOT APPLY TO YOU.